The Lost Secrets of
PRAYER

Discover the Secrets
of True Prayer

Have you ever wondered why it seems "bad" things happen to you? Do you find yourself asking for just "one more" thing? Do you feel your prayers go unanswered? Or when they are answered, do the results bring you only temporary relief or happiness?

You may be surprised to learn that the power of prayer is at work in your life twenty-four hours a day, whether you're aware of this fact or not! So wouldn't it be wise to wake up to what you've been asking for?

Best-selling author Guy Finley presents *The Lost Secrets of Prayer,* your guide to uncovering the secret source of that elusive inner happiness you've been longing for. The true and higher purpose of prayer, as revealed in this ground-breaking new book, is not to appeal for what you *think* you want. Rather, it is to help you awaken from the illusion that stands between you and seeing that everything you need is already here now. Discover these age-old yet forgotten practices for self-awakening and watch how all of life will begin working just for you.

About the Author

Guy Finley is the author of over eight books and books-on-tape, several of which have become international bestsellers. His writings are found in public libraries throughout the United States and his work is widely endorsed by doctors, celebrities, and leading professionals. He has enjoyed numerous successful careers, including composing award-winning music for many popular recording artists, motion pictures, and television programs. From 1970 through 1979, he wrote and recorded his own albums for the prestigious Motown and RCA record labels. Guy is the son of late-night talk show pioneer and radio celebrity Larry Finley.

In 1979, after travels to India and parts of the Far East in search of Truth and Higher Wisdom, Guy voluntarily retired from his flourishing career in order to simplify his life and continue with his inner studies. He now lives in southern Oregon, where he gives ongoing talks on self-development.

To Write to the Author

Guy Finley lives and teaches in southern Oregon, where he speaks twice weekly about Higher self-development. If you would like to write him about this book or wish more information about his other works, please send a self-addressed stamped envelope to:

Guy Finley
P.O. Box 10P
Merlin, OR 97532

Visit Guy Finley's Life of Learning Foundation web site at:

www.guyfinley.com

Take part in his discovery-filled monthly chat room discussions, enjoy excerpts from his books, and get the latest news on continuing developments and special in-person appearances.

The Lost Secrets of
PRAYER
Practices for Self-Awakening

Guy Finley

1998
Llewellyn Publications
St. Paul, Minnesota 55164-0383

FIRST EDITION
First Printing, 1998

Book design and typesetting by Rebecca Zins
Cover design by Anne Marie Garrison
Cover photo © Makoto Saito/Photonica
Editing by Astrid Sandell

Library of Congress Cataloging-in-Publication Data
Finley, Guy, 1949-
    The lost secrets of prayer: practices for self-awakening / Guy Finley.—
1st ed.
      p.   cm.
    ISBN 1-56718-276-3 (pbk.)
    1. Prayer.   2. Spiritual life.   I. Title.
BL560.F56 1998
291.4´3—dc21   97-51713
                                                            CIP

Llewellyn Publications
A Division of Llewellyn Worldwide, Ltd.
P.O. Box 64383, Dept. 276-3
St. Paul, MN 55164-0383, U.S.A.

Printed in the United States of America.

To Reveal the Concealed

What is Truth?
But the moment revealed.
What is life?
But God concealed.

—GUY FINLEY

The being who has attained harmony, and every being may attain it, has found his place in the order of the universe and represents Divine thought as clearly as a flower or a solar system. Harmony seeks nothing outside itself. It is what it ought to be; it is the expectation of right, order, law and truth; it is greater than time, and represents Eternity.

—HENRI AMIEL

Contents

Foreword

Recently, I read an article in a popular magazine reporting new discoveries about how the human brain develops. Researchers had uncovered an intricate and wonderfully elegant process by which unimaginable numbers of nerve cells form a network through quadrillions of connections. These connections are not formed randomly, but follow an inborn "wiring diagram." How the directions for following this wiring pattern are delivered, however, is far from clear, for the sheer numbers do not add up by our calculations: Mathematically, there simply aren't enough genes to provide the innumerable instructions required. What's more, this is not designed as a self-contained process. It is intended to unfold in conjunction with experience in a sort of dance, in which appropriate input from outside must be received at certain critical times to initiate the next step. For example, the retina of the eye must be exposed to light during a specific developmental period. If it is not, the brain connections for seeing simply are not made, and the capacity for sight is lost.

As commonly happens when scientists speak of such discoveries, the investigators interviewed for the article expressed awe at the beauty and perfection of the entire process. They were stunned, they said, not that things occasionally go wrong, but that so much of the time they go right.

Anyone with any imagination at all is also stunned to learn about such findings—especially when one considers that the process these researchers are studying is just one of thousands, perhaps millions, that take place in the human body alone. Add to that the myriad processes occurring all around us, such as photosynthesis . . . the balance of nature (which worked pretty well before human beings began "improving" on it) . . . and the evolution of the universe itself, with its continuous birth and death of stars and galaxies, in a scale of time, space and sheer power that is inconceivable to the human mind.

How could anyone observing even the simple events of everyday life—the bursting forth of spring, the structured activity of the industrious ant, or a cat instinctively nurturing her first litter of kittens—not sense the existence of some great Intelligence underlying the cosmos? Even the atheist, who attributes it all to "chance" and "simple mechanics," would have to concede that those laws of chance and mechanics must be prodigious, indeed.

Surely at some point every human being looks and wonders at it all. And with that wonder arises an innate wish to somehow connect with that Intelligence, so that it becomes a living expression within one's own life. This wish appears to be universal, for anthropologists tell us that every human society yet discovered has had some form of religious belief and practice. Even so, for any one individual to make that Higher connection has always been difficult—has always required a voluntary effort—has always called for some sacrifice of the self to make room for Something Else to enter.

For people of today, with our outer-directed, intellectually oriented, noisy lives, making the connection is more difficult than ever. We're pulled outward into the world of position, possession, and pleasure, and away from any kind of inner experience. The religious instruction that is available tends to be mechanical in nature, emphasizing the social aspect of worship. But the connection to the Higher can only be forged by an individual, alone, and within the deepest recesses of the self. The sincere but frustrated seeker who, with little direction, has tried and failed and tried again asks, "Where am I going wrong? Some grand design appears to direct every aspect of the world I see, except for my own life. I'm confused and unhappy; powerless to bring about the events I'd like, and unequal to dealing with the things that do happen. Is it possible for me to make a connection with something Real and Permanent that can help me make sense of it all?"

Yes, it is possible to make the connection. And fortunately, help is available. Methods are known. They have been passed down from generation to generation since the dawn of human consciousness. And they are revealed here, in this groundbreaking work by Guy Finley. Guy tells us, "We're talking about earning the rights to share in the Secret of the Universe." You see, those rights *must* be earned. They *can* be earned. And you will learn how in *The Lost Secrets of Prayer.*

Basically, the process Guy reveals in this book involves a change of perception. After all, this Higher Intelligence or Creative Principle must express itself everywhere—in every blade of grass, in every breeze, in the movement of the tides. It must permeate everything, including ourselves. Why, then, do we not perceive it? The blockage is *within* us. It *is* us. It consists of the wall of thought that traps us in the limited world of our own imagination and blinds us to Reality. We simply do not have eyes to see what is always there. And this is what Guy provides: practices for changing "eyes" (or "Is") so that the blockage can be lifted and the connection not so much made, as finally revealed.

For many, prayer simply involves asking for what seems to be lacking; and for many, this kind of prayer feels like enough. It may even bring comfort and a sense of being protected. But the kind of prayer Guy describes is of a higher order. These practices for self-awakening actually transform the individual's life. Once transformed, the person never again feels the need to expand his old world by any acquisition, for he has been released from the small world of his own making to enter the complete world of Reality itself. The purpose of true prayer, as revealed in the powerful insights that are the body of this book, is not to appeal for what we think we want. Rather, it is to bring us to the point where the barrier is dropped, which prevents us from perceiving that everything we need is *already* here!

I believe you have never come across anything quite like the material that fills the pages that follow. As you study it, you will recognize that this material does indeed reveal precious lost secrets. Yet the methods Guy offers are so simple and straightforward, you will immediately understand how to integrate them into your everyday life.

The Truth does not hide from us deliberately. If we do not sense its Presence in our lives it is we who are the cause. There is something we do not understand. And in our misguided efforts to provide for ourselves the happiness that

Truth alone bestows, we actually strengthen the very mis-understanding that is keeping us from what we want! The sometimes shocking insights and simple suggested practices offered in this book shed much-needed light into this state of unconscious self-compromise. And with this new light is born a whole new understanding, One that doesn't so much dissolve life's barriers as show they were never real in the first place. The Uncompromised Life follows.

—DR. ELLEN DICKSTEIN

Welcoming Words About What This Book Will Teach You

Picture three people seated at a luncheon counter during a busy noon hour.

One man stares at his half-eaten sandwich as he aimlessly pushes his potato salad from one side of the plate to the other. He can't stop thinking about how, if he'd had just one small break in life, he might have amounted to something really great! And how cruel it was of his new boss to remind him of his shortcomings in their heated meeting an hour ago.

Seated next to him is a well-dressed woman. She's rushing to finish the last bite of her chicken salad combo, chewing it at the same pace as her own racing thoughts. Her mind is working on the details of an upcoming production meeting that she'll head for the first time in her career.

And just two stools down from her is a retired man who has just ordered Tuesday's soup special. On his face is a growing smile because he's looking across the counter from himself where a young mother sits holding her one-year-old child. Her face is only inches from her baby's and she's saying something much too softly to be overheard. But the gentleman watching knows love when he sees it, and he steals a little bit of the moment's warmth to bring into his own heart.

If we look closely at these three brief snapshots of life, taken from the moments of three completely different people, we'll see there is one great invisible Truth running through each of their lives . . . as well as through our own:

Our experience of life, for either the joy or sorrow
of it, is determined by what we are in relationship
with in each moment of our lives.

Let's see how this Great Life-Principle applies to the first
man at the lunch counter. What is he in relationship with
as he sits there? Among other things, he's in a busy room,
music may be playing around him, the aroma of food fills
the air. At this exact time, from another perspective, he's
whirling around on the earth at six thousand miles an hour
while he sits on his stool. All these elements, and countless
others, are aspects of what he is in relationship with in this
moment. But, think about this, please. The one undeniable
fact is that it is *the nature of what he is in relationship with*
within *himself* that is actually determining his life experience. Can you see it? This man is being hounded by his
own thoughts of regret, laced with resentments and self-
doubt. His experience of himself, and what he is relating to
in the moment, *are one thing.*

And what about the woman next to him? What is her
fundamental relationship in the moment? She is mingling
with an unconscious mix of mental excitement and fear
born of flooding expectations. Whirling questions demand
her attention, asking what if "this?" and what if "that?"
until she feels herself caught up in a dance that she can neither walk away from nor enjoy!

And finally, when the older gentleman shared secretly in
the mother's affection for her child, isn't it obvious what he
was in relationship with? He was in momentary relationship

with the mother's overflowing love, which touched his own receptive heart, and the warmth of this love was his experience of himself for that all-too-brief moment.

Hidden in this important discovery—that our experience of self is determined by whatever we may be in relationship with in the moment—is a timeless Principle. It is a great Truth with an important story to tell about the true nature of prayer, its secret purpose, and how to find Real Life.

There are some areas in our lives where we know we have power, and then there are others where we know we do not. For instance, it is not in our power to make anyone else understand the need for God, but it is in our power to see where that person's misunderstanding is punishment enough. Still more to the point, and amplified by what we know is our powerlessness to change even one other person, neither is it in our power to change the way this world of ours turns. But it *is* in our power *to change the direction we are facing* regardless of the way this unwilling world may turn. And this choice changes the world for us because it changes our relationship with the world. But what direction are we to face? Which is the right one? Most of us have been spinning around most of our lives trying to figure out just *that!*

Finding the direction to face begins, as it always has, with turning to look *within* you. But please don't make the mistake of rushing ahead to any conclusions such as "I already know that." If you do this, you'll close the door of a whole new understanding about to be opened to you. There is always something Higher than our present perception, and there is great freedom in realizing this essential fact of life; it allows you to remain open to the ever-new and higher relationship that God wants to have with you.

As we've learned, our present experience of life and of ourselves is the secret effect of our inner relationships. The result of our interplay with those thoughts, feelings, and endless energies is responsible for our ever-becoming sense of self.

Also within us lives and resides Something Greater than the content of all these fluctuating forces; Something within which these energies and their psychic forms dwell, but that is Itself not a part of them—just as a house may hold many diverse furnishings, yet remains greater than and apart from these pieces situated within it. This indwelling Greater Something is an aspect of our True nature in God—a spiritual energy that is *in* all things yet not *of* them. It lends to each of us the power *to be aware* of all these various parts of ourselves and how their ever-changing relationships serve to continually create our fragile sense of self. It is within *this* awareness of the *actual nature* of our present self that Real Self Change, real spiritual rebirth, is made possible. How? Because this new level of awareness first reveals what we are in relationship with and then empowers us to change it.

Think for a minute. Hasn't *every* lesson in life been trying to teach us that the only thing troubling in our lives is where we've been wrongly invested in some relationship or another? Examine your own life for the evidence—including the fact that we don't learn these vital life lessons because we're still living in unconscious relationship with something within us that rejects them, something that refuses to see that our outer lives are a perfect reflection of our inner-relationships. Attempting to change our life experience without changing the forces creating it is like hoping your own echo can give you the answer to your cry of "who am I?"

Do you need more proof? Then I ask you: what is suffering the pain of loss except having been in unconscious relationship with something that you mistook as being permanent that was only temporary?

What is the heartache of betrayal other than having invested yourself in a relationship with someone or something you thought could be depended on, but couldn't be?

What is any sense of disappointment if not the bitter fruit of some relationship with expectations gone sour? And fear, anxiety, hatred, and even self-loathing could not press their ugly lives into our own without our being unaware of our hidden relationship with them. And as we awaken to the truth of this, which ought to be our first prayer to God to help us to do, we are, within this developing new awareness, delivered from being driven to look in the same senseless direction we've been facing all of our lives. We discover there's no point seeking the Real Life our heart desires within these tentative relationships, which have been unconsciously presented to us as having been all that we can be. It is here, at this point of self-awakening, that the true longing for a relationship with God begins. And this longing is always answered because the heart that recognizes and walks away from life's false relationships *is already in relationship* with the Truth, and therefore receives its reward.

There's a popular love song that has become a modern-day classic. I believe that it became successful because its simple lyrics reflect this one change of heart that has the power to change everything else. The song tells of a person having been through—and finally seeing through—a set of relationships whose apparent emptiness brought him to the inner point of longing for only one special relationship. The words say:

> I've been a lot of places in my life and times. I've sung a lot of songs. I've made some bad rhymes. I've acted out my life on stages with ten thousand people watching . . . But we're alone now and I'm singing my song to you.*

Now please allow me to paraphrase the writer: "My life has gone through countless ups and downs—all the things that life brings to one and then takes away—and look where it's brought me: this moment when no one else is around and that's the way I want it. There are no more stages for me, no fascinating lights, no wish for applause. In fact, at this moment, no one but you and I know that you and I are alone together and that I am singing my song to you."

There is no pretense in this lyric. The person is open and honest, alone and vulnerable and receptive, longing for one true relationship beyond both the influences and the rewards of this world. Since the first lover longed for the First Beloved, this is the essence of prayer.

* "A Song For You" by Leon Russell, © 1970 Irving Music Inc. (BMI).

The essence of this book is about awakening *within* yourself *to* yourself, so that in the Light of this new and higher inner awareness you may start choosing in favor of—and truly praying for—the one relationship in life that is Life itself. The insights and practices in this book will help you open your inner eyes to *see* how being unconsciously vested in these impermanent inner relationships keeps you spiritually asleep. This sleep from which you must awaken is not a power greater than yourself, but only a certain *false sense of it that you've mistakenly come to accept as being your life.*

God is not missing. He has never been out of reach, any more than your heart dwells outside of your own body. But He has become obscured, covered up so as to be out of sight. Self-awakening, which takes place within self-seeing, is the Great Uncovering. It is timeless work, with timeless rewards that come with removing what is standing between you and God's Life.

Your life is not intended to be a weary walk through an unwilling world. We are, each of us, a part of a Great Invisible Willing that is not only totally for our well-being, but is actively seeing to its fulfillment moment to moment. We are not alone. We are not forgotten. And even though our circumstances may have convinced us differently, we are not without everything that we need to be content, confident, compassionate, and simply happy.

These words are carefully chosen. They are neither wishful sentiment, nor are they an attempt to persuade. These truths are self-evident . . . which the ideas you're about to read are intended to reveal.

one

When you sincerely enter into prayer, you will come forth with all your prayers answered; but a hundred prayers that lack sincerity will leave you still the bungler that you are, your work a failure; prayers said from habit are like the dust that scatters in the wind. The prayers that reach God's court are uttered by the soul.

—Hakim Sanai

The Root of Real Prayer Revealed

Spiritual stories reach us and teach us in ways beyond the words used to tell them, and reading them with a receptive mind and open heart allows us to take part in each tale in such a way that its story becomes our own. When this happens the special spiritual lessons that each character learns reaches the place within us it's intended to. The truth of it strikes home. And we know it.

1

Please listen to me. Don't be afraid to let the truth strike you. What does this mean? Whether in a simple truth tale like the one you're about to read, or in a moment of great personal crisis, don't fear what life is trying to show you about itself and about you. Welcome it! Yes! Don't resist anything that threatens to pull the rug out from under our feet. Welcome it! Why? Try to see the wisdom in this. We should be thankful to find out that we are standing in the wrong place!

One example of standing in the "wrong place" is depending upon the undependable within ourselves or others. Then, when the reality of our shaky situation suddenly springs up before our disbelieving eyes and we start to take the fall we get angry, blame-filled, or depressed—which is yet another wrong place to stand, guaranteed to lead to another fall. The point is that we live in a constant struggle to keep everything that doesn't fit into what we think life is supposed to be about at arm's length. That's why I say you mustn't be afraid to let the truth strike you. It is not dealing the blow that you think it is dealing. Truth always heals, even though it may hurt at first.

Truth always heals, even though it may hurt at first.

Once there was a very talented young girl who began displaying great artistic promise by the time she reached age seven. Her parents, naturally wanting to help their child develop this special gift, decided to enroll her in an art school for exceptional children.

When the fateful first day of school arrived, after going through the necessary goodbyes, Celeste walked into the classroom where her new studies would begin.

Once she had found a place to sit and had started collecting herself from the shock of being in an unknown environment, she looked around the room. About a dozen other boys and girls roughly her own age were seated in a kind of elongated semi-circle facing the front of the room where the teacher was standing.

After exchanging a few smiles and expressing some encouraging words of welcome to the children, the teacher began handing each child his or her own unusual looking easel, along with some colored marking pens. Celeste was excited and scared at the same time, but before she could figure out how she really felt, the teacher finished handing out supplies and began instructing the class.

It was less than a minute or two before Celeste's attention wandered out of the room. She felt as though she didn't need to pay attention. After all, in her mind she already knew everything that the teacher was saying. So she found something to look at just outside the window that was more interesting. The teacher would say, "Celeste, Celeste, pay attention." But Celeste had more important things to think about.

Finally, after about an hour of verbal instruction and a few demonstrations of some elementary techniques, the teacher said, "All right, children, you may now draw any subject you wish, but here's what I would like you to do based on the principles that we have discussed. Draw a natural scene of some kind that should include trees, perhaps a rock, and maybe some flowers in the sunlight."

About an hour later, the teacher walked around to view Celeste's work, and she wasn't drawing at all what the children had been instructed to draw. Making a mental note to herself, the teacher walked around a few more times; gave a few more general instructions to the class; and asked a few children a helpful question about their artwork, continuing to encourage them.

After a while, Celeste, like all children, was busy drawing on her easel, but increasingly she was looking over to see what everybody else was doing.

She could see that one girl has painted a beautiful tree crowned with a simple sun and set off by one simple flower. Celeste was struck by its simplicity, its beauty. So she looked around some more to see more of her fellow students' works. Then she looked back at her easel and began feeling uneasy. She was troubled by what she saw on her canvas. So she started to put more color on it. She worked a little harder at her assignment.

Now, from time to time the teacher says to the class, "Would any of you like to ask any questions?" A few children do raise their hands and she goes over and helps them. But Celeste asked nothing. She was just working harder and harder at getting more and more color onto her easel. And the more Celeste worked, the more she looked at her easel and the less what she saw pleased her.

Finally Celeste stepped back from her easel and dropped herself, heavy-hearted, into her desk chair. Meanwhile, the rest of the children were talking amongst themselves, laughing, enjoying the creative moment, and busily looking at each other's easels with obvious excitement.

The good teacher, watching all of this take place, and having waited patiently for the right moment, walked over to Celeste and said, "How are you doing?" Celeste looked down at the ground. The teacher, attempting to draw her out, asked again. "Celeste, I'm talking to you. How is your painting coming along?"

After a moment, Celeste looked up at her and in a half-apologetic, half-defiant tone said to her, "Well . . . I don't like what I made."

The teacher smiled at her and said, "Yes, of course," and she waited there for a moment as if anticipating something more from Celeste. But nothing else happened and she started to turn away.

Then Celeste, catching her mid-stride, says, "But teacher. . . ." The teacher turned around and smiled again as Celeste finished her sentence, "What can I do?"

Pausing for the desired moment of effect, the teacher says, "Well, Celeste, there's really nothing you can do."

Somewhat taken aback by her teacher's surprising answer, Celeste looked down. The teacher was still standing there, and the other children can see that she's clearly waiting for something. But a moment later, when she again started to walk away, Celeste shot her hand into the air as if to ask a question and stop her at the same time. "Teacher, please!"

The teacher turned around, knowing that the moment she was hoping for has come. "Yes, what is it dear?"

Celeste looked up and said, sincerely, "I don't know what's wrong. Won't you please help me?"

The teacher smiled gently and responded in openly encouraging tones, "Yes, Celeste, of course I will. I'd be happy to." And reaching into one of the many folds in her large apron, the teacher pulled out a special eraser made just for that kind of easel, and in less than three seconds she wiped Celeste's whole slate clean.

You see, Celeste did not understand that her easel was fully erasable. It was the first time she had ever worked on one like it. There was no way for her to know that everything she'd drawn wasn't indelibly done. At her young age, she couldn't understand the exciting possibility of being able to start over with a clean slate, because she didn't understand the dynamics that could allow for such a fresh start. As powerful a lesson as this one hints to us, it isn't our key one. Here it is:

What do you see when you look out on the world that you've made?

The part of the story where Celeste said, "I don't like what I've made," then, "What can I do?" and then finally turned and said, "Can you help me?" reveals in one pure and simple instant the real root of prayer. Now, to complete the lesson, allow me to ask you: *What do you see when you look out on the world you've made?*

Are you like Celeste in her first hours, when over and over again, you look around and you can see there's beauty; you can see that there's such a thing as unconditional love, as true compassion; you know these wondrous things exist all around you, and then you look at the world you've made—what do you see there?

You must not turn away from the canvas that is your consciousness, although that's what we want to do. The first thing we want to do is convince ourselves that there is some missing color, something else that we're going to do to that ugliness before us that's going to somehow transform it so that when we look at it we won't feel pain, emptiness, or loneliness.

> You must not turn away from the canvas that is your consciousness.

Every man, woman, and even child, at a certain age, looks out and says, "I don't like the world I've made for myself. Look at me. I'm so many years old, I've got this many things, I've got so many plans, but no matter how much I add to the canvas of my life, it doesn't change what I see." Of course it doesn't change. It can't. Here's why.

The world that you look out on—and so often see turned upside down—that world *is within you.* That person who you don't like running into, that strained relationship in any unwanted moment, *is not outside of you.* The reason that you can't get along with other people has nothing to do with the other people. Sure, they're rude. Sure, they're cruel, spiritually asleep, aggressive, all those things—but so are you. Your feelings about the world you see, with all of its confusing colors and schemes, are all reflections of your own internal life. You meet and see only yourself wherever you go. Nothing else. And that's such an important lesson. Can you handle looking at the world you've made? Will you let it strike you?

How many of us feel ourselves trapped in life? You know the drill. "I only have four hundred dollars to my name! Or . . . I only have four hundred million dollars . . . and I feel trapped!" The world that has you feeling trapped is the world you've made in your own image. There is no other trap! The world that has you feeling confined or sorrowful, the world that has you angry, the world that has you rushing—every piece of it has its original counterpart in you.

Let me show you something that might make these last few points clearer, as well as indicate how we can learn to ask for something Higher than what is our present handiwork. Let's arbitrarily divide the whole world into two groups.

In one group there are six and a half billion human beings. And, I don't know, let's pick a wild figure, maybe a hundred twenty people in the other group. What do these two groups represent?

The first group is the world at large. And this mad society is indeed the reflection of our own internal misworkings. It is the making of a people who, in seeing the fractured, misshapen disharmony of the world they've made for themselves *don't* turn and say, "Can you help me?" Do you know what they do? When they look out and see a world they don't like their response is . . .

"Well, I'll just go faster!" Or . . .

"If I can somehow get my hands on more!" Or . . .

"I must learn to sharpen my cunning so that when I trick people into giving me what is theirs they'll thank me for it." Or, when all else fails . . .

"I must find a new distraction; some new form of excitement!"

In one way or another, this is what six and a half billion human beings do daily. Now, let's expose these self-deceptive solutions for what they are. Each must miss the mark because, as yet, these billions of individuals don't understand the real aim of life. They've yet to discover that *faster* is not higher; that *more* is not deeper; that *cunning* is not intelligence, and *excitement* is not love.

What about the second, smaller group of men and women—perhaps you're wondering what makes them different? How do they stand apart from the spiritually sleeping masses?

Simply put, these rare individuals have begun to see that going faster in life does not take them *higher*; that "winning" is not the same as having something *deeper*; that increased cunning has nothing in common with the confidence of real *intelligence*; and that excitement is a poor substitute for *love*. And as the truth

> **F**aster is not higher, more is not deeper, and excitement is not love.

of their finding strikes home, so does its transforming power. Little by little, just as Celeste was moved in her story, they too turn and begin asking, "What can I do about what I see?" They recognize that what they see before them as their lives and their world—the reason they are asking, "What can I do?"—*is as it is because of what they are.* So comes the gradual understanding of the hidden meaning behind the great truth that "*You are the world,*" a Truth spoken by all the ancient wise ones through the ages that, when embraced, holds great promise; or if rejected, punishment. While he was alive, the brilliant philosopher and world teacher J. Krishnamurti never tired of stating this tell-all Truth as "The observer is the observed."

This brings us to the key point we've been working to reach. Allow the truths we've uncovered so far to help you see into its hidden meaning as deeply as possible: *In order for prayer to work for someone, that person has to understand what prayer is really for.*

You may think that you know what prayer is for, and perhaps you do have the right idea. But ask yourself, "How many thousands of prayers have I made in one way or another?" How many of those thousands of prayers have you made that go something like: "Oh please, fix this." "Oh please, help that." "Oh please, bring me some money, or rid me of this nightmare." You've made many plaintive prayers, right?

Within us there is something that prays for what it knows not.

Now, how many of us have made a prayer and had it answered, only to find ourselves in the position where our next set of prayers were to somehow change the very condition we had just prayed into our lives? Maybe an example or two will help clarify this point. "If only I could get my superiors at work to notice me, maybe give me more responsibility, then I'd get that raise!" "Oh, I feel so unappreciated by others, perhaps I should volunteer to be the chairperson of the town committee for lamp post painting, then I'd count for something." Whatever it may be that you've asked for, a short time later you wish you hadn't! How about this: "I'm so lonely. . . . If only I could learn to dance maybe I might meet someone interesting." Then you meet that psychopath out there in the bar someplace, and now you're still lonely and, on top of that, you're scared to answer your own phone for fear that it's him calling!

The point of these examples is that often the basis from which you are now saying, "Please change this" is because the very thing that you prayed to have come into your life has. Now, what does that mean? This happens to us and we don't see it: Within us there is something that prays for what it knows not. Would you ever consciously pray for an answer that turns into a problem? Of course not. Nobody does that. Or do we?

"All my life I've prayed, and I've prayed, and I'm still . . ." —tie all the lessons together now—"and I'm *still* looking out and seeing a world I don't like." Translation: I'm still anxious. I'm still frustrated. Still pressed, angry, rushing, whatever it is.

Don't miss the point here, as millions of (newly hatched) skeptics do. Just because I have made all of these prayers and they haven't been truly answered doesn't mean that there isn't a God. It simply means that I don't know what I am praying from and for. Obviously I don't know what I'm praying from. If I knew what I was praying from, I wouldn't pray something into my life that turns out to be the next thing I have to pray about. That's number one. More importantly, I don't know what I'm praying for. If I really knew what to pray for—if I really understood what prayer was for—I would receive those things that increase the quality and contentment of my life. And from my enhanced well-being, I would look out at my world and say, just like God said, "All is well. It's good."

There are very important points here. First, we are conditioned to believe in ourselves as prayers who actually know what we need. Second, it is ingrained in us that we know what it is that we are to pray for. The nature of this social-religious conditioning runs deep, but the light of our own awakening awareness to our actual condition begins to change us. It brings us, albeit slowly, to that moment in our own story when that weary little girl or boy within finally learns to say: "Can you help me, please?" Because, and I'll explain this in a few ways, in the moment when Celeste asked the teacher, "Can you help me?" a number of things changed. For one, Celeste had to realize that she was not going to be able to make what she saw before her into something she wanted to see. When she asked her teacher, "Can you help me?" it was an admission. It was an *admission.* Consider all that this request implies.

"Can you help me?" is not you thinking you're going to get your way. Rather, "Can you help me?"—when it is sincerely spoken or felt in the heart—is both an admission and a confession that you don't know how to make your world into one you want to see. You need help to do it. And what happens in this moment of admission? Let's look at Celeste's life first, and then we'll get to our own.

In that moment of admission, what she really said is, "I *need* to converse with you. I want to see it the way you see it." Even more important than this spoken request is the unspoken invitation behind it. You see, any admission that invites correction also asks for *relationship*. You can't have this sort of admission without asking for and being willing to receive the special relationship it implies.

Here's another view of this important idea. Say that I come to you and I admit something of my own lack of understanding. The very moment I come to you, especially after I've first pushed you away, I have asked for a new level of involvement with you—a relationship that couldn't exist before because of my pride. My request for this relationship is my admission, and this admission is my wish for correction. Because of it, in the very moment it is acted out, I am brought into relationship with something that I formerly was not in relationship with.

Any admission that invites correction also asks for relationship.

Now, make the beautiful connection: in relationship is communion. And this new communion begins in our story with "Can you help me?" And then comes the answer, "Yes, I can."

That beginning of talking, that commingling of ideas, is just the bare beginnings. What happens eventually is that the teacher, who represents God in our illustration, and Celeste, representative of each of us, begin to mingle at that moment of admission. This new relationship, this communion, allows the student to see what the world can be. And that's a whole different story.

We have in us, the way we are, this idea that somehow or other we are going to be the ones who make the world that we see work. This notion runs very deep and is strengthened in us, in part, by what is its partial truth. We're very reluctant to see that for all of these years, and all of the things that we've been doing—with ourselves and for ourselves—that every day we still see what is ugly or unwanted on the canvas of our lives.

If we're fortunate, there comes a certain point when we know that we can no longer afford to refuse what we know we see. And if we'll just endure these first difficult stages of true self-seeing, new Insights follow whose Light rescues us by revealing that we've been unconscious captives in an invisible circle of false strength. And false strength is any power we have to go looking for after it's needed!

Think about it! What good is it to find a solution—some seeming strength—that doesn't really resolve our problem, but is just another form of secret self-deception? What I'm getting at here is that outside of its power to help someone temporarily feel better about the weakness that just overtook him, what good is the "strength" of being able to endlessly explain himself to himself? Or to "intelligently" justify some deliberately hurtful act toward another; to tell himself that *this* time he's learned his lesson and how he won't ever do *that* again—but then he *does* do that, or something like it, again.

We *all* do this until one day a certain miracle takes place. And our studies have been leading up to this breakthrough moment. On that one bright day this same person cries out:

"It's extraordinary how I always find myself looking for the strength I need after my moment of need . . . and how it always manages to appear after the fact to tell me everything I should have done! Therefore, I will no longer call upon that strength—or any other kind of strength that I must add to myself. In fact, what I want now has nothing to do with any of those things I've been deceiving myself about. What I really want is a New Self."

Rare are those of us who come to pray for a New Self, because few reach the point where we say, and really mean, "Can you help me?" This is because it's impossible to ask for a New Self, for a New Life, for God to be our life, until we have played ourselves out—until we've taken all the colors that our false nature can muster, and thrown them up in every possible combination on that canvas there, and realize that no matter what we do, we can't get it to be pretty and stay that way.

What good is it to find a solution that is another form of secret self-deception?

The world of your making is so wearisome. Just look how you have to make it over, and make it over, and make it over. But that's not the worst part. The worst part is that you start running out of things you can imagine to make it into! Then what happens—and it has to happen—is that this same self-creating nature then turns on itself. It gets vicious with itself and it gets vicious with everyone else for the pain that it is inflicting on itself. And as it does that, it closes itself off forever from saying, "Can you help me?" because it can't help itself. And when it can't help itself, it closes the circle from help coming in forever by denying that there is anything outside of itself, which it does with self-loathing and self-hatred. We've all known someone who, certain that the world has cruelly set itself against him, sets himself against the world, thereby effectively setting into motion all of the self-created negative forces that prove to him that his hatred has merit.

So we reach the point where a person starts to understand that there truly is an order to this process of real prayer, because for prayer to work it must begin with *a genuine request*. This genuine request has to be based *in reality*, not in wishes, hopes, and dreams. It can't be based in wants. It can't even be based in ideals. For it to work, prayer must have what it needs to work—the uncovered heart, the exposed heart. This heart can't be lied to anymore by the mind, which says, "*One day* you will be beautiful, wise, or strong." At that point, when reality produces our request, this request is the same as the Way. And the Way, if one adheres to it, is the same as approaching what amounts to a number of invisible interior doors. And incidentally, these doors really exist. Christ said, "Knock and it shall be opened to you." This special knocking has to do with sincerely saying, "Can you help me?" Surrender the self at each door on the Way, and then the door opens. This will happen to you, for you, if you'll persist sincerely with your wish for a New Life.

Work with the following higher understanding until you can see the truth of it *for* yourself *within* yourself. From this

> **For prayer to work it must begin with a genuine request.**

moment forward start seeing that when, in a fit of unhappiness, you feel like you weren't made for this world, at that moment the "you" that is speaking made that world. Your task in prayer, and with prayer, is to reach a very simple, quiet state—the very simple admission of "I don't like the world I've made. Can you help me?" Then, just like the teacher did for Celeste in our story, your slate will be wiped clean. Celeste didn't know the teacher could do that, but the teacher was just waiting to be asked. So is God just waiting to be asked.

When God begins wiping clean the slate of your life, it doesn't mean He passes on to you a certain strength that now makes you a believer in yourself as someone who can create great things. That "strength" that you feel flowing into you as you enter into relationship with God is you leaving behind the level where you are identified with the weakness that made you a victim of everything you encountered, including your own thoughts. So, it's not growth the way we imagine seeing ourselves growing. There has always been confusion surrounding the idea of what it means "to grow" spiritually, but perhaps never as much as in these present times.

Real spiritual growth is a kind of passing; it is the old giving way to the New because we no longer want what we once were. In that quiet passing comes that Self which was always there before, which you are now at last communing with. Every single longing, every prayer a person ever utters and reaches for, always has to do with Something within; Something somehow felt to be just beyond reach, and if only they could get through that door and stand there, all would be well.

That's the spiritual path. It's within you. And you must make the journey. But to make the journey you have to be on the Way, and to be on the Way, you must understand the request that begins it. Give up in the right way. Learning to surrender yourself begins with learning to see *the need* to surrender yourself. The rest takes care of itself.

Special Lessons for Self-Study

One of the unseen barriers is that we are approaching the problem of changing ourselves from something that only knows to approach the problem with the very ideas that created the problem in the first place.

One aspect of your inner work is to be willing to see the limitations and the suffering inherent in living from the ideas you have and hold on to about yourself.

The power of our prayers is increased proportionately by the degree to which we have played ourselves out and know it.

For prayer to work it must begin with a genuine request based in reality and borne of the uncovered heart, the exposed heart.

Admitting you cannot change yourself is the true beginning of self-change, for this admission is also an invitation to the Higher Relationship that changes everything.

Prayer that craves a particular commodity—anything less than all good—is vicious. Prayer is the contemplation of the facts of life from the highest point of view. It is the soliloquy of a beholding and jubilant soul. It is the spirit of God pronouncing his works good. But prayer as a means to effect a private end is meanness and theft. It supposes dualism and not unity in nature and consciousness. As soon as the man is at one with God, he will not beg. He will then see prayer in all action.

—R.W. EMERSON

two

T̲he telling question of a person's life is
whether or not he is related to the Infinite.

—CARL JUNG

To Touch the
Timeless Truth

At first he wasn't too thrilled about
the whole idea. After all, who wants to
leave the comfort of home for several nights
of sleeping on rocks and eating dehydrated
stews? Not to mention missing five straight
days of his favorite morning cartoon shows.
But his parents gently insisted, and the more
he heard about the special activities this
adventure camp offered for kids his age,

the better it sounded to him. And so it was settled. The last precious week of Paul's summer vacation would be spent going through what his dad kept calling a "growing experience!"

During these wilderness camps for kids, young children go away for a few days at a time into completely natural settings to help them develop greater self-confidence and self-reliance. This was how Paul found himself in the mountains with about two dozen strangers: other boys and girls roughly his age, along with an experienced guide and a couple of junior counselors.

These are not easy times for seven- to nine-year-olds. It's scary away from home! Strange sounds fill the night and strange sights round out the rest of their time. So it wasn't that unusual that all the kids moped around, whining and complaining, all of them, that is, except one—Paul.

Being connected is an essential part of self-awakening and prayer.

About the second day into the adventure, one of the junior counselors noticed that little Paul just didn't seem to be having the same problems as the rest of the would-be campers. Taking him aside from the rest of the kids, she said to him, "Listen, I was wondering. All the other children are either scared or complaining, while you just don't seem to be disturbed at all, which is great! But still, I'd like to know," she added almost as an afterthought, "what's going on with you?"

Paul smiled that kind of sheepish smile children turn on when they've been caught with their hand in the cookie jar.

Looking up at the counselor, he spoke quietly, "You promise not to tell?"

"Well, I guess so," said the junior counselor, now completely baffled about what in the world this little boy could be talking about.

Having established the rules, Paul reached into the inside pocket of his parka and pulled out a powerful pocket-size walkie-talkie. Looking back up at the counselor, Paul said, with obvious pride, "My dad gave this to me just before I left so that I could talk to him whenever I needed to!"

In case the lesson isn't as obvious as it's intended to be, this little boy in our story was calm because *he was connected.* And the whole idea behind being connected provides us with a very broad scope of studies through which we can discover many wonderful things about the true nature of self-awakening and prayer. So, let's begin, and please think through all that follows so that we arrive together at a higher understanding.

If someone asked you, out of the blue, "Where's the king?" and then continued to prompt you for the most obvious answer, you'd likely reply, "The king is in his kingdom!" A likely answer, because in this world, the king is usually found right there in his kingdom.

In the spiritual world, the Almighty is in His Kingdom, too. It would fit, wouldn't it? The King is in his Kingdom.

Now then, *where* is that Celestial Kingdom? You know the answer—at least intellectually. You've heard it, or read it, a thousand times, but most likely its secret "hiding place," as well as the hidden meaning of it, has escaped your understanding. So, where is this Kingdom of kingdoms? *This Kingdom is within.* So far, so good. Let's review: The King is in his Kingdom; the Kingdom is within.

Unfortunately, we have all manner of wrong ideas about this Kingdom. Look. The King is in his Kingdom. The Kingdom is within. But if this Kingdom *is* within each of us, as we're told it is, then why aren't we New human beings within it?

Let me restate this vital point of study.

If the Kingdom is within, which it is, then *within what* is this Kingdom of kingdoms? The Kingdom is *within me.* Yes or no? Now we've got simple logic. The King is in his Kingdom. The Kingdom is within. The Kingdom is within me.

Now we've come to an important juncture, so do all that you can to make the transition with me into this next higher line of thought. The Kingdom is within me—but now we'll change the idea to state the same fact using a slightly different term: The Kingdom is in "I." Aren't you "I"—do you understand? *The Kingdom is in "I"* . . . What I am; how I *know* myself.

The way the present religious world has it set up, the kingdom is "out there." It's a future issue; perhaps someplace you're going to go when you die—if you've paid enough money, if you do enough "good" deeds—meaning that the Kingdom exists for you, either as a place exterior to yourself *or* in a hopeful idea about yourself. The vital lesson in focus here is that the Kingdom *is within "I."* If in fact—and this is the fact—the Kingdom exists within "I," and the

King is in His Kingdom, which He is—there must be something amiss with our present "I" because we're not in touch with our God as we're created to be. Did you make this critical leap with me?

Something about this present "I," this small self that I presently take myself to be and that I understand myself through, is obscuring the King within, the Truth, Christ, Reality . . . you fill in the word.

The King is in his Kingdom; the Kingdom is within.

There is something in this present "I" of ours whose presence and dominating qualities absolutely exclude us from living the Higher Life we are each created to enjoy. If you understand this observation, then you have to ask yourself this very important question: "What is 'I'?" And this question is not the same as "Who am I?" Nor is it simply an intellectual pursuit. You must arrive at the point where you see that God and His Kingdom somehow dwell within what you are—within "I"— but that somehow this "I" that you know, live from, and draw your sense of self from absolutely does not know anything about it. It only knows the ideas it clings to when it tries to save itself in dire moments, which is not good.

Let's examine this extraordinary finding. Let's do some conscious investigation into the nature of what is "I."

We can start by showing that presently, "I" for us is little more than a special kind of idea. Apart from our own temporary ideas about ourselves, we don't really have a permanent "I" that we live from. The "I" that we say the Kingdom should be within doesn't include this Eternal Kingdom, otherwise we would all have and live within a comforting sense of our own timeless existence. Everlasting life would be here, *now*. It would be self-evident. We wouldn't have to struggle to seek it, or work to create it through fevered imaginings. Clearly something is wrong. And what's "wrong" is the "I," and this "I" is an idea. Oh! What we've just come to! What we need to begin to do is to change our ideas about ourselves.

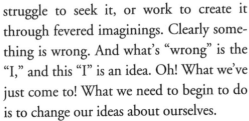

We need to begin changing our ideas about ourselves.

What does it mean to grow up? Do you remember the first time you knew you had to grow up? Wasn't it something like, "If you want that fifty-cent allowance, you have to take the trash out once a week!"

Or do you remember that terrible death knell that rolled right through you when the teacher said that dreaded word, "Homework!" *Homework!* "Oh, no! You mean I can't watch Superman? No more Wonder Woman?"

So, growing up involved, in the beginning, *responsibilities*, didn't it? You had to have new responsibilities. And if it seemed that with each new age came a new set of responsibilities, it's true. We grow up into ascending levels of responsibilities, each reflecting another new and higher ideal. A big part of growing up, of maturing, has to do with entering into relationship with certain ideas that pre-exist the one who is growing.

How about other ideas connected with growing up? Remember this one—that first time you thought to yourself—"I think I love her?" Those powerful emotions surging within you? Whatever the age, it's a startling experience.

"Wow! I never knew a relationship could be like this!" And you fall in love. But the heart of this relationship—and all others—was created before the beginning of time within a beautiful idea called Love!

Then, as you continue to grow up, perhaps finding a dedicated life mate, you realize one day, "Ah, now I'm married, with a child of my own"—or whatever it may be for you in a time of self-evaluation. You realize: "Now what? I'm still growing up. I've got kids. They have needs that outweigh my desires. I'll have to make sacrifices." Sacrifice is an idea, an unspoken mandate seeded in the heart of all creatures before the word was ever spoken.

On and on the life can grow, developing and transforming itself until, if you keep going, you may one day get to the point where you realize that what's missing in your life is a certain depth of compassion that lies beyond your present reach. And this unrealized compassion of yours has nothing to do with just giving something away. It has to do with the next degree, the next level, the next depth of relationship. If you're true to your finding, then you must continue growing up. You have to, little by little. And then comes the question: Into what are you growing up? The answer may surprise you because it appears that our personal maturation is measured by increasingly higher levels of ideals that we grow into. But this is only half of the story, if that.

We do not just grow up into ideas; ideas grow into us. Understand that this process of growth we're investigating here is really something *coming into you*. It is the marriage of something that already exists with something readied for that Union. Think about it.

The nature of responsibility exists before the first human being does a responsible act. The nature of relationship exists before the first person puts the hand of a lover together with his or her own. And compassion exists before the first human being ever said in kindness, "Can I help you with that?" or, "Let me not burden you with my problem." These states of energy exist independent of their earthly expression. They exist before any human being became the so-called owner of their quality. These are ideas I'm giving you, aren't they? I'm giving them to you because, combined, they reveal something very important for you to understand if your intention is to change the "I" from which you presently live.

Let's review briefly: our ideas and our sense of self are really one thing that we experience as being our "I." Do try to see this. Our ideas and our "I" are one and the same. In other words we know ourselves only through our ideas about ourselves. Without new ideas our "I" can't change.

Now, our own physical senses help to produce the illusion that we're connected to a world that we see and experience as being separate from ourselves. But the truth is that we *are not connected to* any perceived condition: what once happened to you, what you hope will happen, what any exterior condition makes you feel like. You perceive yourself as being connected to the world. However, know that you are not connected to the world, but *to your ideas about the world that your senses have defined.*

Your senses report to you that the world is "out there" and you're feeling the way you do because of the way things have turned in it against you, the cruel action that this person perpetrated upon you, so forth and so on. However, *you aren't connected to the world, but to your ideas about the world,* which your senses tell you exist outside of you. Ponder these last few special points. Your time spent in such study will be well rewarded. Here's why.

Real Knowledge is, and always has been, critical for real spiritual growth.

Our senses cannot give us new ideas. This is why Real Knowledge is, and always has been, critical for real spiritual growth. Only with new insights that naturally align us with the greater unseen Reality are we naturally empowered to come upon, and have come into us, New Ideas to know ourselves by and in. And there is much at stake in coming to understand these New Ideas now before you, as the next paragraph will reveal.

Your senses report to you this physical world in which you now live. These physical senses tell you that "you" are apart from "me," that I am apart from all "others," and that they are apart from whatever it may be that they want something from. On and on it goes. All of our ideas about this life are constructed on what the world is that our senses tell us we are in. And these same ideas can never get beyond themselves, because they are the product of the world our senses perceive. We are their captive, in the real sense of the word, until we learn to see that these self-limiting ideas are only part of the whole story.

Now, what is one of the most limiting ideas that our physical senses report to us?

The idea of *Time*.

"Time! Where's it going? I can't hold onto anything, try as I might. What I won, how you felt, the way she looked, the things I love—like a strange river's torrent that vanishes from view as it rounds an impassable bend in a shadow-filled gorge—what is *past* just disappears, leaving only memory in its wake, itself subject to the ravaging passage of time. I'm without power here! That's for sure! I'd better turn myself around and start looking in the other direction; better look ahead to the future. But wait a minute, I don't believe in what *will be* so much anymore because tomorrow never really comes; only more of its empty promises."

So, if you're following me, here's virtually every person living in a moment in which everything seems to flow *out* in one direction. They can't quite get their hands on it because it's gone. By the same token, everything else in their lives appears to be on its way—only whatever that's to be is not here yet!

Have you ever seen a run-off stream from a brief rainstorm hit a dry desert floor? The sands swallow the water without leaving any evidence of it even having been wetted. *That's* the flow of time from our point of view. Try to see it.

We dwell in the house of the perfectly present moment.

Our life's experiences lie in the sand of what we call the past. The moment they're gone, they *are* gone. You can observe people all the time desperately digging through what was, hoping to put their hands onto the life they knew that's no longer in sight. Do you know what they're doing? They are digging in the desert, trying to find those brief, passing waters that once refreshed their lives. But the waters are gone.

You can see this, too, if you'll look. When the digging is too painful or unfruitful these same people try looking forward. They turn around to face a hopeful future and say, "Well, maybe I'll find what's missing by looking in this direction." This is the point. Incidentally, these truths about the way we see our world, and our actions because of it, help to explain why Buddha called this a world of suffering. *Everything* in this time world of ours is temporary, passing, fleeting. Everything in *that* direction—gone. Everything in *this* direction—not here yet. But here we are. *We're* within this present moment and have no way to hold anything. What was is gone; and what's to be hasn't arrived!

But please pay close attention now, because we're about to turn this idea around. On the other hand, isn't the definition of Eternity something that "has no beginning and that never ends?" Yes, it is. This is the Alpha and the Omega. The Truth is—and what our senses can't grasp— that our being dwells in the house of the perfectly present moment. We live in *now*. However, our physical senses report to us this undetected present moment as a kind of unreality, an untouchable medium through which all things flow, but in which we can get our hands on nothing, not even ourselves. It's true, isn't it? Aren't we always looking for that elusive sense of "I"?

Everything we're looking for in life is ultimately a search for something through which we can come to know, and hopefully possess, ourselves. But where are you looking for

"I"? Aren't we always wondering, "where did it go?" Think about it. "He *did* love me!" Or, "Oh, no! Where did it go?" Or, "Wait, I'm sure it's coming!" The point here is that "I" is never real, it never remains permanent for you, because it, the sense of yourself, is always connected to that which has just passed or to that which may be coming. Please, work at considering these important ideas until they show you their wisdom.

So, "I" is presently the way we understand our experience of the present moment through our senses. And this fleeting sense of "I" is forever hoping to pull the water out of the sand; to somehow make something that isn't real yet real so that we can get our hands on it and say, "I am real! I do exist!" But we can't quite do it, can we? It's a bit like a nightmare, isn't it? We are always almost there.

Have you ever seen a circus acrobat who balances spinning plates on poles while racing around from one to the other to keep them falling? That's what our present sense of "I" is like. What makes it wobble? You can fill in the blanks, but here are a few examples. "Oh! look, he's leaving." "Oh! she's changing." "Oh! I'm losing everything." or "Oh! I hope it's going to work out."

Now, listen to this wonderful new (yet ancient) idea. *Everything that ever was or ever will be* already *exists.* When the Supreme Being created the heavens and the earth, the entire thing was made from beginning to end, complete. In Ecclesiastes we are told: "I know that whatsoever God doeth it shall be done forever: nothing can be put to it nor anything taken away from it."

So in God's world, all already *is*. It is an established creation with all possibilities. The past, present, and future are not in time because they are eternal creations always already extant. But within *our* present level of awareness, that limited consciousness granted to us through our senses, there is for us this sense of the movement of time. Our senses report to us that what is past is gone. You hear people confirm this incomplete view of reality every day and in

Everything that ever was or ever will be already exists.

a thousand ways, usually followed by "how I wish I could get 'it' back." However, truth studies strongly suggest that "it" is *not* gone. Rather, the "I" which you and I live from—with its temporary nature—is incapable of perceiving anything other than itself through reflecting upon experiences that belong to the stream of time.

Now, can you look at that idea and see that inside of it there is the possibility of a new "I"? Can you look and say:

"Wait a minute. This whole business, my whole life, it's always about trying to get hold of something that's "coming"—or to hold on to something that's "passing." I meet everything and relate to all events from a sense of passing time, a sense of self that includes my feelings of loss and the hope of gain. All of my relationships are based in this one pervasive and often painful idea. I'm learning that who I really am *is and always has been* a part of the Eternity that God created 'in the beginning.' And . . . that all of that time I'm so worried is gone, or so concerned that it may not come, that all of it—my past and my future—was made in the beginning. Who *I really am* cannot be lost. It is within my power to understand that remarkable passage from Ecclesiastes that tells us: "He hath set Eternity in the heart of man."

Now, if this new and higher order of self-understanding seems like a tall order to fill, listen to me. It isn't! The same God that created the Ages gave you the wherewithal to understand your place within them. Let me show you.

Recall now our short story about the little boy, Paul, alone out there at the wilderness camp. He was calm, wasn't he? What was the source of his peace and composure? *He was connected.* So, the first part of these new lessons in learning to live from your Higher Self and the prayer exercises that attend them is that the next time you feel yourself becoming agitated, simply notice what idea you are connected to. Look how simple that is, if you'll do it. Here is one small example.

Unconscious conclusions become your tragedies.

You are driving down the street and you notice that you're feeling depressed. Or maybe you're feeling anxious. That's the *first* step: to see yourself; to be awake to what's going on within you. Ordinarily, the nature that feels negative, the self that embraces that stressed state, looks to itself to explain why it feels like that, which does nothing but advance the process. Now you have some new information. *You're in this condition because you're connected to what you're connected to.* Period. And what you're connected to in that moment is nothing but some self-limiting idea you have of yourself, an idea that's telling you who you are and defining you based upon *its* incomplete perception of life. In unheard whispers it claims, "unless so and so approves of my actions they're worthless, which means I am too." Or, "If I lose that account, or that relationship, all will be lost." Mistaken ideas delivering wrong conclusions—unconscious conclusions which become your tragedies. Now can you begin to see how much Higher Help is just waiting for you in these new self-discoveries?

Your spiritual work is to begin the deliberate process of bringing into the present ideas you have of yourself—those new ideas that actually show you the limitations and suffering inherent in that same idea you're unconsciously living from. Our findings so far, and the point of this important exercise, exclaims *there* is *another kind of "I!"*

You don't have to look to anyone else for your sense of "I"—not in the world's opinion of you, not in any other place you've ever mistakenly looked for it. In fact, in the light of these findings, you must realize the need to stop looking for what is your Self in the world, in others, and in changing conditions. Why? Because when you're connected to that "I"—to that idea—you hurt!

Once again, the exercise is to notice what you are connected to at the moment, and then to consciously bring into that relationship the new idea that *everything is already done*. Yes, it's done. And if there is anything in you that resonates with the idea that you can't make yourself into more than what God has already done, then you have a seed of something Timeless, and you can begin to let that idea have its Life within you.

So the first part of this exercise is to work at waking up to what you are connected to. Then, from within your newly awakened awareness, to see that any painful idea defining you is an illusion; a shadow of yourself cast from other, conspiring mistaken ideas. And now let me explain how prayer can play in helping you to realize this Timeless Life within you that awaits your discovery.

I urge you to take time, at least twice a day—though preferably as often as you possibly can—to simply, deliberately become aware of what you are connected to, and then drop it in favor of your wish to have God's Life. Prayer is not about asking for things from God, but first to be with Him, then in Him. That is the essence of prayer. It has nothing to do with gifts. It has to do with awakening to that Being that isn't in time. This is the Gift of all gifts.

Think this through for yourself. If everything didn't seem to be moving away from you—and ceaseless change *is* the nature of time—and if it didn't appear as though everything you long for might still be coming "one day," would you be the way you are? Would you be *who you presently are?* Would you have the sense of yourself that you have right now? Do you see? In a too real sense you are forever seeking "I," seemingly finding it, only to lose it again. The possibility of Real "I" is crowded out by a legion of thoughts based in wrong ideas whose inner clamoring drowns out reality's rescuing message: All Is Done.

To make the journey to what may be called Real "I" within yourself begins with a New Idea. And as we've discovered, this New Idea is not really new at all. It too was made in the beginning, and the whole thing is complete *now*. The King *is* in his Kingdom. The Kingdom *is* within, and this "within" *is* hidden within the New "I" within your God-created nature. And this New Nature must be invoked, welcomed, and invited in.

So when you sit to be quiet, when you're meditating, doing your prayers, or whatever your practice may be, here's a way to invite those true inner changes your heart longs for.

Repeatedly bring yourself back to yourself and then, from within this present self-awareness, realize that instead of being connected to the "you" who is always struggling to get something, hoping to become someone, trying to resolve things—surrender yourself to the understanding that the whole issue of who you are is *already* resolved. Let go and know that Life is complete, timeless, and so are you. Do not go into imagination. The self you imagine will be a secret extension of the self you wish to escape. Everything you need to pray, to wake up, to be new is right there with you without having to "create" it. But our ideas don't report that to us. Our ideas report that we have to do

> **The whole issue of who you are is already resolved.**

something to "get there." The illumined author Vernon Howard stressed to his students the new idea that to succeed spiritually, "there's nothing to do, only something to see." This is the truth. See in those moments that the way you perceive life is what is punishing you, and then let what you start seeing change the ideas you have about yourself. I promise you it will.

Take into your meditative or prayer life the understanding that the idea of "I" from which you presently live is not going to make the Cosmic Connection. You can't have a new mind with old ideas or, as Christ states, "You can't pour new wine into old skins." So the first connection that you need to make is to simply and deeply see that; and then allow these new ideas that you've been given—this new knowledge—to set you on the Path to the Truth that sets you free. Allow these special insights you've received to develop by doing your part to nurture their necessary growth. And then watch what happens.

Special Lessons for Self-Study

For better or worse, the quality and content of your
life experience is determined by what you are
connected to.

You perceive yourself as being connected to the world,
but you are actually connected to *your own ideas about
the world* that your senses have defined for you.

All of us feel we understand, intrinsically, that we are not
meant to be beings who are continually changed into
whatever it is that comes along.

Before you can hope to change any personal condition of
conflict in your life you must first see where and how
you are connected to it.

Prayer is not about asking for things from God, but
first to be with Him, and then in Him.

> You never enjoy the world aright, till the Sea itself
> floweth in your veins, till you are clothed with the
> heavens, and crowned with the stars: and perceive
> yourself to be the sole heir of the whole world, and
> more than so, because men are in it who are every
> one sole heirs as well as you.
>
> —W. J. TURNER

three

Thou dost keep him in perfect peace,
whose mind is stayed on Thee.

—OLD TESTAMENT

Develop the Indomitable Self in You

Prayer is not what you think it is.

The truth is that we have all been given a tremendous amount of information, most of it misinformation—indirectly and directly—from individuals who, without any real interior experience of their own, having either assumed positions of authority or had it granted to them, instruct others about the

41

Way to God. This brings to mind an old Sufi saying: "May God kill he whom himself does not know the Way to Heaven, and yet presumes to show others."

Having such insufficient inner instruction for too many years has predisposed our thinking toward having a very limited, often childish knowledge of what prayer is; of what it's about; of what it's intended to do. Even worse is the thought that this "knowledge of prayer"—along with its potential power and implied relationship—is somehow our possession alone and that the weight of it somehow makes us the center of the universe around which all others should orbit. Such spiritual immaturity is the secret seed of religious fanaticism, a form of sickness that thrives within any unconscious aggressive conviction that others must see life as you do and that pushes you into the life of someone else *who has not invited you in.* To demand that anyone blindly conform to anything is harmful *to* all involved and *for* all involved.

The way to the truly interior life is deeply, necessarily personal.

The entrance into the truly interior life, which is at once the basis of prayer as well as its cause, is deeply, necessarily, highly personal. In the last chapter, we discussed the importance of embracing new ideas in order to invoke the birth of the Timeless Life we seek within ourselves. So in the interest of this Truth we pursue, the following questions should be asked because of the new ideas their honest answers will reveal.

Why is our spiritual life something we practice only in certain places or at appointed times? How come it's almost an inconvenience to have to go someplace for spiritual reasons, such as meetings or services to worship or to study Truth? What makes it so difficult for us to perform our inner practices each morning before we launch into the day, or quietly read a spiritual work before we slip off to sleep? Yet, *whenever* we find ourselves having been just knocked down by life, we *can't stop* crying out, as though there's no way to understand it, "God, where are you? Allah! Why have you let me down?" or "Christ, come into my life and save me, a sinner." What I'm asking you to consider here is why is life divided up into these times where a person fairly burns for a relationship with something Higher, and then, for what is the greater part of his or her life, this same person gives virtually no thought whatsoever to the Celestial?

We must admit that this condition is an accurate description of our present lives. We must be honest. Self-honesty is one of the main-sails that, when opened and allowed to be filled, helps to deliver a person to the safety of Truth's shore. As difficult as it may be, we must be willing to see that the bulk of our present energies and efforts are consumed with pursuing money or authority; with struggling to get people's approval; in fearing how "this" or "that" will impact our carefully laid plans; and all of the rest of figuring out what to do when it appears we're not going to get our way. And oh, how in these moments, do we turn our tear-streaked faces towards the Heavens as though we've never thought to look any other place!

The following may shock you, and I hope it comes as just that.

Everyone practices prayer twenty-four hours a day . . . only they do not know they're praying, nor do they know (and this is the real problem) what it is they're praying for! And this fact of life includes those people who say, "But I don't believe in prayer. I don't have a spiritual practice." A moment's consideration of the following insight proves the truth of this claim.

Expectation is a form of prayer.

Let's look at a few simple examples to prove the point. Don't you walk around hoping that what you've hoped for will happen? Whatever that hope may be for you? "Of course," you would have to reply. "But what's that to do with prayer?"

Hasn't it ever occurred to you that your hope that money's going to come is a kind of prayer to the god of money? Certainly no one deliberately, *consciously*, sits there and says, "Oh please, lord of dollar bill signs, pour yourself down on me." Then again, most likely, some do. Hopefully you don't say to yourself, "Oh god of Mars, strike down this person who said that evil thing about me." But you may be hoping for some harm to befall someone who hurt you. It's possible the wish for revenge may be the momentary point of your life, as it becomes for many when they feel betrayed. So in case this isn't yet clear to you, realized or not, these hopes and wishes, all such similar underground expectations are prayers.

Expectation is a form of prayer.

Part of the very purpose of this book is an attempt to cleave through this huge barrier that exists in the minds of men and women that there is something impractical about understanding the true nature of prayer or—in other cases—to remove an equally large false assumption that they already know the secrets of prayer, in spite of the fact that their lives are basically a series of repetitious acts spent trying to push away recurring troubles. And we all know this kind of life too well!

What you are really praying for is to be able to possess yourself.

Here comes this unwanted feeling and here comes that nagging thought. Here comes this unsettling news and here comes that frightening condition. The thoughts come like storm waves pounding on the shore and you're trying to figure out how to keep from being washed away. How many of us have ever thought, "Why is this happening to someone as nice as me?" We're forever telling ourselves, "I don't deserve this kind of pain! My life is not supposed to be spinning out of control!" So we pray—in one form or another—*for* something that we think is either connected to what we want or *to* something that's greater than the condition we perceive is punishing us. What we don't yet understand is that within these prayers, whatever form they may take, we're praying for something that we don't understand. And this is why life continues to bring us the very things we say we don't want.

What you are *really* praying for, the still-secret purpose for your prayers that you don't yet understand, is to be able *to possess yourself.* Think about it! When you were a small child (it happens to us even as adults!) you went to the beach and a wave rolled in and knocked you off your feet. Then, just as you struggled to your feet, along came another wave to knock you off your feet again! It's a good metaphor for some days in life, don't you agree?

Here comes this condition, this anger towards someone, and it knocks us off our feet; then all of a sudden here comes this other condition rolling in from a seemingly different direction, perhaps remorse for some unthinking cruelty on our part, and it bowls us over just as we're getting up!

There isn't a single person reading this book who hasn't had that terrible helpless feeling of watching oneself hand their life over to an unwanted dark state. You go to bed at night and you're subject to unwanted dark dreams or unremitting scary feelings. You awaken each morning to feelings of regret or defeat about what you have to do even before you do it. But a point comes in all of this when a small but definite self-realization dawns within you. It's clear now. You must stop blaming life for the presence of these dark states and start accepting the obvious truth of your present condition: of yourself you just don't have enough to keep from being washed away. And as this (at first humiliating) new self-understanding grows in you, you naturally start asking life for something new. As slow as it may have been in coming, you're beginning to get the picture. You're now able to see, albeit "through a glass darkly," what is really missing from your life. And your new requests reflect this realization.

"I'm tired and fed up with being the unwilling victim of all these contrary forces that I'm subject to. What I really wish is to unite with something that will give me the strength, the ballast that I don't have of myself in myself. I *need* to find some new sort of strength that will help me to stand up in my own life and allow me to stay that way."

For the record, honest requests like this are rare. The person in denial of his or her own condition continues to ask for more of what didn't help him the last time around—more money, a better body, a new relationship, a better position at work, increased social prominence—on and on it goes, going nowhere. This person hopes against hope that somehow *this* time he'll find that missing anchor that will keep him from being bowled over by the waves of life's events. In one way or another we've all

There are hidden ways to request an unshakable Self.

stood and fallen on similar ground as this. Trying to add ballast to ourselves through acquisitions of one kind or another, only to find that rather than anchoring us, our desires and their seeming fulfillment only tend to make us top-heavy and easier to topple. So now what? Please carefully consider the logic and higher lesson the following insight holds:

If we receive from life what we're asking for, which is *always* the case, maybe it isn't so much that we're unable to ask for the right and rescuing realities as it may be that *we don't know how* to request what we really need. Yes, it's true. But it's *also* true that there are secret ways of asking that you don't yet understand, hidden ways to request an unshakable Self.

The New Testament parable of the prodigal son tells of a young man who, as the story unfolds, originally lived in a pretty good place. All that he needed was provided. But, like many of us, he saw greener pastures outside of his given life and so he leaves it and eventually squanders everything his father had given to him.

Then, one fateful morning, he awakens to find himself having slept in a pig sty and having only corn husks to eat. He looks at himself and his surroundings and says, "I'm an idiot. Why did I leave home?" And at that moment he turns around and goes back home.

The story continues that his father sees him heading back home from this great distance and calls to his eldest son that his younger brother is returning and that he's to go and kill the fatted calf. With this the older brother becomes enraged, saying, "I've been with you all these years. I've given you everything I have, and now this good-for-nothing (you can tell they really cared for each other!) comes home after squandering everything you gave him, and you're giving him the feast! Why?!"

The answer recorded in the New Testament that his father gives him is, in essence: "Because my son was dead, and now he has come back to life. He was lost and now he's found." But let me reveal to you the secret answer within this answer.

What the father of the prodigal son has really said is: "I'm doing this (preparing a welcoming feast) for him *because he asked for it*. By his actions your brother has requested this expression of my renewed love and loyalty. You've been with me all along, so there was never any question of your fidelity. But your brother, he was gone. He was a lost to me, and his wish—along with his action *of turning around* to come home—is a special request to be once again a part of this, my kingdom."

This powerful parable tells us there is a different order of request. Most of us think that prayer is primarily asking for something: "Please do this for me," or "Would you just do that?" or "Why won't you intervene?" We think prayer is somehow connected to wishes centered, one way or another, on ourselves. But, what we're talking about here, what we're attempting to reveal, *is the spirit itself* inside of the human being that is first necessary in order to receive the request that he's asked for.

The "lost" son asked for his new life by seeing that he was wrong and then deciding to return to his home. Incidentally, he did not know what was going to happen to him. And I'll tell you that it didn't matter to him because here's what was going through his mind as he headed back home: "I've been a fool! All I possess is my own mistaken self." And he knew it. Which brings us to the key point: the understanding of his true condition—and the subsequent action he took based on this knowledge—was a form of Higher Request.

What I'm hoping to convey is that there are ways of asking for things that you don't presently understand. And until you do understand how to ask for what you want, what you *really* want, you will continue to ask in the ways that you think are appropriate. You will continue to ask from a nature that doesn't know the difference between what is genuinely good for you and what is not. This is a

huge question for all of us. Presently, the way we're consti-
tuted, our lives are nothing but a series of requests, whether
they're done in a "spiritual-religious" sense or from out-
and-out greed or ambition. We are always asking, and then
not understanding, why it is, despite all the things we've
asked for, our lives still seem to be this proverbial leaf in the
wind.

So let me start with the following. You may later ponder
its many levels of meaning. In this world that you and I
live, *response is request.* We can slightly enlarge this idea by
restating it this way: The way you respond to life is also a
request you make to it. The next few examples will prove
this important discovery:

Someone walks into your home or office and says something to you that upsets you terribly. You respond
with a negative state, continuing to brood or broil
over what's been done long after the offending
party has left. Is your negative state (your response
to the event) not a request that others who walk
into your life that day will see you and treat you
according to the condition you're expressing? Surely you've
seen that like attracts like? And isn't your refusal or inability
to let go of that negativity a request on your part to live
within the condition that now has taken you over? Think
about it.

**Response
is request.**

Perhaps you say: "Well, no. It's not a formal request on
my part to be taken over by a dark spirit. That negative
feeling came in and overtook me."

What you don't realize is that the punishing mental or
emotional condition dominating your spirit has no real au-

thority whatsoever to take you over—NONE! *No dark state has authority over you!* No self-compromising state is entitled to command who you really are! Now, is this higher understanding at work in your life? Most likely not. The odds are that you'll have to admit that virtually every state that comes visiting expresses its life through yours, whether welcome or not. Fear surfaces, you're afraid; cruelty appears, you're cruel; hostility comes, you're hostile; anxiety jumps up, you're uptight. Every response of yours that either embraces or denies the visitation of these self-compromising states is a secret prayer on your part to never possess yourself. Now, in the light of these new and true facts about ourselves, let me ask you: What is it that we're praying for?

We're praying—if we're praying—because we know that we're not meant to be human beings who can be blown this way or blown that way; bowled over and turned into something dark or hateful. We know that we're not supposed to be psychologically fearful, so that we take advantage of other people to free ourselves from our fear. We know, or at least deeply sense, these truths about ourselves. Yet every visiting state that comes, every despairing condition that washes over us, *transforms our life into its own.* When that state turns us into what it is, we are unable to respond to life from anything other than the content and "quality" of that state. Our inability to respond from anything but the quality of that state is the same as requesting all the conditions that are in line with and similar to that negative condition. Are you following me? Because this new finding reveals two very important discoveries.

First, we have an inherent God-given understanding within us that we're not intended to spend our lives being dominated by anything. This cannot be stated strongly enough. Nothing is supposed to dominate us—*nothing!* But presently our lives are nothing but a series of explanations to ourselves about why we have been dominated and how we will never be dominated again. Incidentally, this includes being dominated by what we call excitement, because it always just flips in this world of opposites into the boredom or the depression that follows its receding high. So, here we are day in and day out dominated by one mental or emotional state after another, washed over so thoroughly that there's no difference between us and what has washed over us.

The second part of this self-discovery is even more fascinating. Each and every state that washes over us is replaced with another state that washes over us in the form of a reaction or resistance to the initial state. Thus, we are never truly in possession of ourselves; our lives are secretly spent running through a series of being possessed by these mechanically alternating states.

I wonder if these inner revelations strike you as deeply as they're intended to. Because as long as you and I continue to live from our present ideas, which always involve being able to explain to ourselves why we were dominated and what became of us, we will be victims forever of that idea, of that self, of that "I." Because that life being lived out from this level of consciousness has no real choice, only the illusion of one. Now, if you'll follow the upcoming sequence of mental and emotional waves, you'll better see the truths being revealed here.

Hatred washes over us and it's replaced by some guilt; then guilt is washed away by a feeling of trying to get forgiveness, and the forgiveness is washed away by the next condition. Meanwhile, within everyone's experience, virtually at the same moment all of this is going on, there's a feeling that something is terribly wrong with

We are not intended to spend our lives being dominated by anything.

knowing ourselves from this runaway sense of self. We feel this way about our lives in these moments of lost self-control because we understand intrinsically that who we really are is not meant to be continually changed into whatever it is that comes along! Here's the proof that this sensing is intrinsic:

Will you agree—continuing with our original metaphor—that these negative states that wash over you also roll around you even as they roll you around? Yes, they do. It is as if you've been caught in a rip-tide: you can feel one set of currents pulling you in one direction even as you're aware of other currents waiting to pull you in yet another. Like being in the grip of an anxiety while fear waits its turn to get you even more turned upside down. This essential insight into our inner world raises an important question for us to ponder: If you know these runaway inner states wash "you" back and forth like a bubble rides the tide—that their action rolls you around and around—*what's the hub?* Go slow here. Your careful consideration of what's being revealed here will be rewarded in ways beyond words.

Consider the ground upon which those waves roll back and forth. You know the waves. You're pushed around by them or punished by them. Yet for now, at least, you don't know the ground. The point is that you couldn't know these states as waves *unless there was ground underneath.* You could not have the awareness of these negative states going around and around unless something within you *wasn't* going around and around. This is the nature of the hub of any wheel. This is what I mean by intrinsic nature. That's what I mean by something already being inside of you that is the Unchanging Being you seek.

Next, let's add some additional but necessary knowledge to this study by taking a look at one of the states that visits us. Let's use anxiety (instead of letting it use us!).

When anxiousness comes, would you say that you're in control of your life, or is that anxiety in control of you? Pretty clear, isn't it? Now, do you recall how the previous chapter presented the nature of responsibility, sacrifice, and compassion, and how these ideals we aspire to are eternal in nature because when God made the heavens and the earth, these higher ideas were also made? Well, those states of anger, pettiness, and fear are also eternal. These negative states, like their positive counterparts, dwell in an existence that isn't in time the way we'd imagine.

In ancient times, teachings about the assorted gods and goddesses—Venus, Jupiter, Mars, and the various angels and demons—reflected a certain level of insight into the invisible forces at work in the universe. These myths and stories, borne from intuitive insights, were told to help understand the existence of certain eternal states that were created by the God-Head when he said, "Let there be . . . ." This implies to us that Love, as well as all of the lesser positive and negative states, is eternal. And that the powerful influences of these more eternal energies wash over this planet, penetrating and interpenetrating one another as they do us.

The true state of love can't turn into the hate state. The angel of light can't turn into the demon of darkness, any more than the demon of deceit can turn into the angel of integrity. These states, powerful and eternal, are forever what they are.

At our current level of consciousness, we experience ourselves as beings who have a certain emotional state of energy come into us, which defines and shapes our individuality. But the fact of the matter is that there is no separate self. Not really. There are just these states of energy and the fleeting sense of self that their undetected possession produces. We then fight and resist the state—or if it's pleasing we embrace it—while believing that we're doing something for ourselves, from ourselves, and that we're special for our experience. Then in a heartbeat, because that state isn't really ours and only washes through, the minute its nature has moved on, so does the sense of self that we had derived from it. Now a whole new and unwanted feeling floods in, leaving you asking yourself, "Hey, I'm missing something here. Where did my life—my sense of self—just go?"

We spend our lives in a continual kind of unconscious struggle.

So we spend our lives in a continual kind of unconscious struggle, attempting to overcome our own persistent and painful sense of loss. We search for a way to contact some power to empower us; to make us superior to those states that punish us, or to allow us to hold onto these pleasing states that lend us a sense of ourselves as being powerful or loving. Now the truth is that you are meant to be more than any of these states. Can you imagine?

Wouldn't it be tremendous if the next time a wave of anger came over you, you were *more* than the anger? Or what about the next time you started to sink into some doubt or depression, wouldn't it be wonderful if you were *more* than that futile state? Think about what it would mean just in our physical world alone. We're cruel to one another because when we get angry or depressed, all we know to do is to express or repress the state. Our response, in turn, attracts exactly the thing we say we don't want. Think about what it would be like to be more than any mental or emotional state. The purpose of discovering your real internal life is to show you that there is something within you that is *already* much more than any one of these states, or all of them combined.

We have the Ground within us upon which waves of states both move and break.

We have the Ground within us upon which these waves of states both move and break. But rather than living upon and from the Ground that these waves break over, we continually identify and find ourselves in the ever-rolling waves. As long as we continue to find ourselves in these waves, the only thing that we will be is dominated. We'll continue to feel ourselves as victims, longing again and again to possess ourselves, all the while thinking in a response to some wave that just broke over us that, "if only I had 'this' or owned 'that,' my life wouldn't be so unsteady."

Think about what it would be like for you to begin asking to live from God's ground. To stand upon something unshakable. How do you ask to live from that ground that knows itself as part of the whole, yet isn't washed away by it?

Can you see how down to earth such a question really is, even though it deals with heaven? If not, then you can begin seeing its value by asking yourself if you've ever given yourself away; sold yourself for a crumb; been the fool *again*? Then ask: wouldn't it be nice to never again be washed away by any state that compromises your real life? This is what I'm talking about. But you have to ask for it. You have to learn to ask in the "right" way for this kind of Help—and the "right" way *is the spirit you ask from.*

The beauty of this new request is that as you begin to do this special internal work, you find that there are actually ways that you can work at being more than the state. But the way that you work at being more than the state is by becoming aware of its presence within you and, while remaining aware of it, working consciously to neither express nor repress it. When you refuse to give yourself over to any state that ordinarily dominates you, for the first time you are conscious of the state and the ground it is rolling over. Do you see this? Here's a spiritual fact that will help you to develop this necessary new and higher self-discernment.

All of your emotional states are visitors. They are not *you.* They are not selves. They are part of your self only to the degree you identify with them, which then turns you into that expressed self.

So, when this psychic visitor comes, your ability to recognize it as a visitor does what? All of a sudden there's you *and* the state. There's you and the condition that before has dominated you because you didn't

All of your emotional
states are visitors.

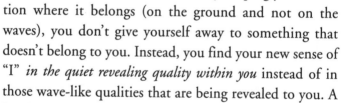

recognize it as being a visitor. You thought it was something you had to go along with because you thought it was "you." And by keeping your attention where it belongs (on the ground and not on the waves), you don't give yourself away to something that doesn't belong to you. Instead, you find your new sense of "I" *in the quiet revealing quality within you* instead of in those wave-like qualities that are being revealed to you. A brief review will serve us well.

In every moment there seems to be a "you" and the appearance of these visiting states, whatever their qualities, rushing over and through you. Ordinarily, as each mental and emotional state moves into you, its nature defines you. You're unaware in these moments that you have within you a Being that is changeless, that is indeed timeless. But you can't ask for this wonderful, truly empowering internal Life to be yours as long as you continue to identify with every single emotional state that wanders through you. So it's necessary to work at self-detachment. And this effort of conscious detachment is a special form of prayer in two ways.

First, as you can begin waking up to the presence of these visiting states and work to deliberately detach yourself from their inner influences, you won't lose yourself to them. This is an elementary but powerful form of self-command.

Second, as you become newly aware of yourself in this way, you'll also *contain the visiting state.* This conscious sense—of being both containment *and* its contents—is the proof there is something "higher" than that visiting state. Not only does the higher contain the lower, but it also reveals the presence of another Self whose lofty nature may be in one world, but that is not of that world at the same time. Please ponder this deeply. You can understand all that it implies because the truth of it lives within you. Find it there.

Start asking for a relationship with what can't be washed away by doing this specialized work upon and within yourself. Learn to ask for something that is Permanent. Ask for something that doesn't shake. Ask for something that doesn't turn into its painful opposite by learning to recognize and detach yourself from what you've always mistakenly assumed was yourself. This is the kind of powerful prayer that proves itself even as it provides proof that within you dwells the Indomitable. Work at it every moment.

Find that immovable ground that is inside of you. Learn to live there by working to not let your life be lived out by visiting states.

Special Lessons for Self-Study

Every man and woman on this planet prays twenty-four hours a day without knowing it because no one understands that *expectations* are a secret form of prayer.

Freedom from what is *unwanted by you* begins with awakening to what is *unseen within you.*

In this world where you and I live, response is request.

All emotional states are temporary visitors, not selves. They are mistaken for self through a process of unconscious identification with their temporary appearance in the psychic system.

As long as you continue to identify with each temporary emotional state passing through you, it cannot occur to you to even ask for the truly empowering internal life where the Eternal One begins.

We are not human beings having spiritual experiences; we are spiritual beings having human experiences.

—PIERRE TEILLHARD DE CHARDIN

four

Whenever a mind is simple, and receives a divine wisdom, old things pass away—means, teachers, texts, temples fall; it lives now, and absorbs past and future into the present hour. All things are made sacred by relation to it, one thing as much as another. All things are dissolved to their center by their cause, and in the universal miracle, petty and particular miracles disappear.

—R. W. EMERSON

New Knowledge that Awakens New Prayers

There was a young man who used to go to the gym every Wednesday and Saturday because he enjoyed working out and using the equipment they provided. One day when he was there, as with all the days that he'd been there before, he finished his exercises about the same time as a certain older man who would shower and groom at approximately the same time. It just so happened that their gym lockers were only a space or two apart, so they often sat on the same bench while they dressed.

On this particular late afternoon, the young man was seated there and the two of them were into the final stages of putting on their clothes. This was the moment he dreaded most and sure enough, he looked over and the older gentleman was doing the same thing that he'd been doing for two years: he was sitting there, bent over, desperately trying to shove his feet into his shoes that he didn't untie! It was a Titanic struggle. Do you ever do that? He was struggling and then stomping, wiggling his foot first this way then that, jamming it in. When this didn't deliver the desired result, he'd wedge his finger in the back of the shoe as a shoehorn, only to pull it out a second later while exclaiming some kind of bad word. And then he'd do the same thing again and again!

When are we going to learn that what we are doing just doesn't work?

The young man always watched this dressing drama in amazement, because every time, after the fellow had fought with his shoe for about four minutes, he would look down, shake his head, pull off what had barely gotten on his foot, take the offending shoe in his hands, untie it, put the shoe on his foot after he made an adjustment of sorts, and finally tie the laces in a double knot.

The young man had watched him go through this routine for what seemed like ages without ever saying a word. But today was different. He just couldn't take it anymore!

He had begun to see it in his dreams. When he'd be driving to the gym he'd be thinking about this ordeal that he knew the man would be going through. So he just couldn't keep his mouth shut anymore. He said, "Sir, I don't mean to pry, but I've been watching you every Wednesday and every Saturday for years now trying to squeeze your feet into those shoes." He paused to collect his mounting emotions. "And every Wednesday and every Saturday you go through this same struggle until you say some expletive and then you take that shoe off, you untie it, and then you put it on your foot." He took a measured deep breath and continued.

"Sir, I don't mean to pry, but, you know, there *are* other ways to do that," he said as he motioned his head and eyes at the man's other shoe, which was dangling there half on, half off of the man's other foot. "Why don't you just take your shoe and untie it to begin with? And besides which," he paused once more, slowly shaking his head as if trying to sort out his own thoughts, "I don't understand something else. Every once in a while I've actually seen you squeeze your foot into the shoe. It's in there, and then you take the shoe off anyway! Please explain this strange behavior to me!"

The man said, "Well, son, it's not that complicated. The reason that I have to take the shoe off is because when I'm getting my foot in there what happens is that my sock gets twisted on my big toe. And it's too uncomfortable like that. I can't stand it, so I take the shoe off to adjust the sock."

Truly confused at this point, the young man said, "Well, now I really don't understand! If that happens most of the time, and the other times you can't even get your feet into your untied shoes, why don't you just do it the right way the first time?"

The old man looked at him as though he felt sorry for any such person who couldn't comprehend the obvious, and then he spoke: "Well, son. One day it may work!"

We all know people who insist that one day they'll get it right, don't we? But let's get closer to home. When are we going to learn that what we're doing doesn't work? Day in and day out we fight to accomplish something that, even when we manage to accomplish it, it is rarely the accomplishment we thought it would be. I defy you to tell me this isn't true. Yet, amazingly enough, it's also the truth that in spite of these results we're still trying to squeeze "this" and "that" into our lives! We're going to make "it" work no matter what! And we've got so many new ways to try to squeeze those "shoes" onto our feet. The next trip. The next plans. All these different ways to accomplish the same nothing.

It's critical that you understand what you're being told here is not the voice of gloom and doom. Just the opposite is true. The sole intention of these self-studies is to help bring some much-needed light to bear upon your present understanding—a whole new kind of light in which it becomes abundantly clear that virtually every single moment *you are receiving what you pray for.*

What do you do with that? Here's what most of us do. We exclaim: "It can't be true! I'm hurt, I'm scared, I'm angry, I'm anxious. No, it can't be true! Besides, I have enemies, people who are trying to hurt me. Are you saying that I'm praying for that? I live in a world that doesn't understand me in the smallest way. Are you saying that's something I'm asking for?"

What I'm telling you is that there isn't a split second in this world that you don't get what you're praying for. Can you get away from yourself for a second and see that:

a) It may be true, and

b) If it is true, which I'm about to show you it is, that in understanding this invisible truth-in-action there's some genuine hope for changing what we've been receiving from life?

There is genuine hope, a genuinely brighter future, in understanding that the way you feel right this very second *is* an unseen request. And if that's true, which it is, then this new fact also reveals that it's possible for each of us to discover what it is within us that is making these requests. In so doing, we learn to change them in order to change our lives. But first, let's back up a little bit.

> Every single moment you are receiving what you pray for.

God is tremendous. In His infiniteness, in the infiniteness of the Truth of that which is All and Absolute, there is tremendous compassion. The expression of this compassion is that every single human being is actually able, consistently, in one form or the other, to take part in creating the life he or she wants.

The problem with this gift of being self-creative is a spiritual one. Most people don't know they have an invisible nature within them that wants something *for itself* that's against their own true best interests. As difficult as it may be to reconcile your hopes for a brighter world through some kind of cosmic intervention, God does not make allowances for the sickness this unconscious selfish nature spreads throughout society. He is not concerned in the way we imagine that the man way over there, or the woman nearby, is living under such-and-such conditions or may have been treated in this or that way for so many years. There is discernible evidence for this last statement; one which, *because* of God's compassion, is also self-evident. So do try to see the truth and inherent wisdom in the following facts.

> **O**ur lives create and reflect the level of our understanding or the depth of our ignorance.

Every person ever thrust into some seemingly overpowering circumstance is (more than) equally empowered to understand that what he or she receives in those life moments amounts to their *individual* life experience; and that what they experience as their individual life has to do with that level of life's possibilities that they embrace and ultimately express. To say the same thing using different terms: *each* one of our lives creates and unerringly reflects the level of our understanding or the depth of our ignorance. Connect this fact with the God-given gift of being able to experience our own being, through our ongoing awareness of it, and we are indeed as empowered to change our life experience as we're willing to assume responsibility for it.

What this tells us is that the Truth isn't going to walk through our front door and say, "Listen here! You've *got* to get this lesson." That's just not the way Heart of Reality works. Yet, it is, because all along Truth has been shouting: "Wake up! *Your life itself* is all the reason in the world why you *need* to learn the life lessons right in front of you."

God is absolutely equal opportunity. Absolutely fair. Absolutely compassionate. Into every single one of the souls sown onto this planet is that which gives them the ability to produce from their requests what they receive. And there is no reception outside of the requests that you make. So, if your heart's heavy, or you're angry, or you're frightened, or you're impatient, or you're nervous, or you're scared, or you're caught up in money, or whatever it is that you do every single day, you have requested the pain that comes with those requests you don't know you are making.

If you can see the whole picture here, it tells a story we may not want to hear. Nevertheless, if we'll open our inner eyes and ears, it explains so much. God doesn't make allowances for the fact that you're conditioned and don't know it; that you receive from your conditioned nature what you do that punishes you; and that from this conditioned nature producing these pains, you then make new prayers that bring you new punishments. All this goes around and around only because you don't yet understand yourself.

The person who doesn't know, and accepts what ignorance permits, receives what ignorance requests. Now, let's take the word *ignorance* and change it to better express its meaning in the context of this study: The person *who does not know himself,* and who accepts what his life is like without *self-*

knowledge, receives from life what the absence of that self-knowledge requests. There are no excuses. Absolutely none. "Reasons" may abound, but there are no excuses for living in the dark. But we don't, or maybe more accurately, we will not, see ourselves.

Could the man who kept trying to shove his feet into his shoes understand that on Wednesdays when he heads for home in his car, he's angry for most of his drive-time because he fought with his shoes? And that all the way home he's receiving what he asked for? And that when he's driving home and he's angry, and someone cuts him off, and he flares into an explosion and does something dangerous—perhaps endangering his life or the life of someone else—that he requested this very moment of danger that may actually snuff his physical life out? If you spoke to him to point out these truths, just as I'm revealing them to you, he'd say, "No, I didn't! It's this world with crazy people in it!" *But the real answer, the unseen, unwanted one, is that it's a world with* you *in it.* It's a world animated and activated by a certain level of self-understanding that does the same things day in and day out without understanding the role it plays in the conflict, confusion, and misery it creates. That's why you and I must work to become a different kind of being.

Please picture in your mind the following scene, thinking about what you see. Two thousand years ago on their days of worship, prior to the services, men and women would stand around in small groups and discuss their mutual concerns. If we could eavesdrop, perhaps we'd overhear them talking about the evil Roman Empire or the unfair rate of exchange the gold mongers were making on the temple steps. Surely some would be arguing with others about the benefits of eating certain vegetables and grains. Then, when the bell would ring announcing the beginning of the religious service, all would summarily put on their most devout look and enter the temple, acting like they were there to pray and to worship God. When the service was over, they'd all depart their separate ways to take in a meal someplace, usually gossiping amongst themselves along the way about some piece of news, maybe complaining how hard life is. And during this whole time—*before, during, and after* what each considered the appointed hour of prayer, every single one of these people was praying with every word that came from their mouths, with every action, for exactly the life that he or she was struggling to bear. That's the word, isn't it? To "bear" this life. "God help me from this life that I have to bear."

We are empowered to change our life experience.

God help you to see that the life that *you think* you have to bear *is* the life you are bearing. There is no other life than that!

As a quick exercise, the next time that you find yourself anxious, angry, depressed, or feeling dominated by any negative state that's come into and over you, what would happen if right in the middle of that seemingly unwanted moment you heard a voice in your head saying, "Ah, this is what I was praying for." Wouldn't that be quite a shock? And a healing one at that, because it would be the Truth.

Let's look at another example of this unconscious prayer in action.

You wander into a conversation, and you listen to someone talk about something maybe she's getting out of life that you're not; or perhaps you are drawn into a discussion about something that possibly threatens your future. So you leave this conversation anxious or frightened, trying to understand: "How come I feel the way I do?" The next moment, to answer this developing ache, you ask yourself, "What can I do about it?" You have now just sown a prayer into what was sown into you during that last dialogue. And then—because God is good and God is gracious—you get what you've asked for: An answer *you give yourself* that promises to take your fear away. Only it can't! Because any answer you buy into to free you from a fear is itself a secret extension of that fear. This Truth partly explains why Christ said, "Resist not evil."

Cooperate with your own continuing self-development every day.

Once you begin to welcome the higher lessons revealed in this book, which is the same as understanding what should be your first order of business on this planet, you won't waste a minute getting on with your inner work. We are each supposed to be cooperating with our own continuing self-development every single day—our lives dedicated to increasing the kind of understanding that allows us to begin having a relationship with Something that is already quite complete, Something that is forever showing us something wider, broader, and more meaningful. So do what you must to remember this: your prayers are answered every microsecond to microsecond. Allow this realization to dawn within you. It will establish within you, *for you*, a whole new set of priorities. Instead of wanting different *things* from life to make you happy, you'll begin to want *to be someone who is different.* This New Wish, along with the new inner work it calls for, helps to put you in relationship with that which is already perfect.

There is a peculiar self-compromising condition that exists in the human life, hidden in the depths of our uncharted psychology, that has been taught about in various spiritual schools throughout the ages, but perhaps never better illustrated than within one particular story recounted in the New Testament. It concerns the truth about these states that wrongly dominate us, revealing at once both their secret source and power over us.

Perhaps you already know the story. Near the end of Christ's life, he was talking to his disciples. In so many words he told them, "The good news is, I'll be back. But for now, it's necessary for me to go through some very difficult times. More than ever, you must stay wide awake now."

The point is that when He told them what was going to happen to Him, one of His closest disciples, Peter, leapt to his feet, saying with great passion, "Oh, Christ, I'll never let that happen to you." In so many words he assured Jesus, "Regardless of the cost, I'm with you until the end because of how much I love you." At this point, Christ replied: "Peter, before the cock crows on this fateful day you are going to deny me three times."

Now most likely you aren't aware of the following difference, and I'm certainly not a scholar in Aramaic, the original language of the New Testament, but when Peter spoke of his love for Christ he's quoted as using a particular word for it whose context expresses a certain kind of emotional state. But when Christ spoke of love he used the word translated in Greek as "agape," a word whose meaning implied a timeless state of unconditional Love.

So, here's Peter saying "I love you" even as Christ was saying to him, "Yes, but do you love me as you are professing—or in the way I've been trying to teach you about as being *The Way?*"

The story goes on to show that the only kind of love Peter knew was a kind of emotional state that had taken him over so completely that he believed he was a true lover of Truth. He was absolutely convinced, in the grip of this love he thought he had for Jesus, that come what may he would never deny Him.

Hidden in this powerful teaching story, and revealed right at the close of its dramatic section, is that up until that telling moment when people began asking Peter if he knew Jesus, *Peter did not know there was no* real *Peter there at all!* Just like you don't know there is no you by the name you give yourself when you're possessed by a powerful state that calls itself you.

I wish these Truths were something that every human being on the earth could understand and *love.* To welcome and embrace them would give this planet the chance to become what it was created for. But with things being the way they are today—with the way *we* are, *which* is *the world*—there's virtually no chance for this growth. Only the rare few are willing to see that the way they presently are, there's no Real Self there at all, just a series of states that gives them something to resist or embrace, to which they say, "I." And this is that same "I" we discussed in an earlier chapter about where the Kingdom of Heaven is not found! Do you remember the lesson? Let me refresh your memory.

The Kingdom is within. Within what? It's within me. And what is this me? It is my sense of "I." Well, if the Kingdom is found in "I," how come we can't seem to find it and live within it? Now at least we can see some of the reasons: The sense of "I" through which we know ourselves is little more than one fluctuating state after another, a conditional psychological entity produced by reactions, which themselves are fragments of past experience.

Please don't let this revelation throw you. In fact, be assured that this new self-realization holds the promise of great inner rewards far beyond the ability of any words to convey.

For one thing, you should be strongly encouraged to learn that after Peter denied Christ three times, *after* that shock that shook him to the depths of his soul, he finally understood the lesson that Christ had intended for him all along.

In the moment of his self-collapse, Peter was able to see beyond any self-supplied shadow of doubt that he was *never* the person he'd always dreamed himself to be. This shock about his "self" was a life-giving awakening. In this worst moment of his life came the threshold to the New and Higher Life now opened to him. Peter suddenly realized that for his whole life he had mistaken his emotional and mental states for being the same as himself. And in this same moment, he began to understand that he would have to free himself of all the false visitors he had taken as himself before the Christ he loved could ever visit him within. Here in an instant was revealed to him the hidden meaning of the inn being full and unable to accommodate the Christ's Birth. Peter knew why old skins can't hold new wine, and more. The veils fell from his eyes.

My purpose in explaining this story's inner meaning to you is to help you see that just as it was for Peter in times of old, neither do you understand that when you are taken over by a state of some sort that it's not real, because *you become that state.* You don't know when you are possessed by something temporary because you are literally its temporary possession. There's no difference between the "I" that it creates in you and the state that created it. They are one and the same.

Now, here's an insight that also hints at a special form of prayer in action if you can understand its higher instruction. Not expressing any negative state is the same as revealing the self that is *not* it. This secret spiritual instruction deserves special explanation. When you don't, when you consciously *won't,* express some negative state, you are literally asking for awareness of a Higher Self. Here's why: as you don't express that state, you become conscious of yourself as the ground it's breaking on as well as the presence of that visiting state. In this moment of new awareness, there's something inside of you, with you, that won't change when the state changes.

Wouldn't you like to know a miracle? First, that God *is*—that His Spirit is eternal, permanent, *the* miracle. That you can experience this miracle of miracles within yourself—by learning to consciously witness the coming and going of these inner visiting states—that's *your* miracle. Approaching this same idea from another angle delivers the same result: wouldn't seeing where you've been losing yourself your whole life be the same as getting close to being wholly self-possessing? Think about it. Isn't that what it means? What is it to not possess yourself? It's to be whatever vagrant state happens to pass through. And I sometimes pray that they're good states because I want to get possessed by joy. Don't you? But the problem with getting possessed by emotional joy is that it either evaporates in the course of time, or it just disappears when the temporary conditions that created it change as they must eventually do. Then you're left there empty, not only taken over by whatever state happens to be next in line, but wondering, "Where did my joy go? What happened to my happiness?" You think it's gone because the "you" that was connected to it, created out of it, has disappeared too. So now you're looking for it again. Now you want to be more! And the whole vicious cycle starts again. "If only I had more money, more authority, it wouldn't leave me!" Yes . . . it will.

> **N**ot expressing any negative state is asking for awareness of a Higher Self.

If the inner discoveries revealed in this chapter sound true to you and you'd like to take the next step in doing the inner work required to help set you free from yourself, here are some suggested ways to begin detaching from the visiting states.

The next time that you're somewhere by yourself and all of a sudden this complaining visitor comes in—you know what I'm talking about, the whining, negative state that wants to complain about the way your life is—remember the secret prayer-in-action we've just discussed: Not expressing the state is the same as revealing the self that is not it. Go silent to that self that wants to hold onto or glorify misery.

Go silent to that self that wants to hold onto or glorify misery.

This act of self-sacrifice is the same as asking God to lift you above yourself—into His life—which He will do.

Here's another way to self-separate. Do you ever speak badly about other people behind their backs? Why would any of us ever want to badmouth another person? Because they must have done something that upset our sense of permanence. Again, a moment's reflection here is worth a lifetime of being self-determining. Dare to *look at yourself* when you denigrate other people, and you'll see that you feel this need to lash out because it seems to you as though they've made your ground shake. The truth is, they didn't make your ground shake. You're just being attacked, visited by a vicious, shaky state. When it rolls through and gets you to say "I" to it, your life belongs to it. *Not expressing, not gossiping, is a form of requesting for yourself something that doesn't need to talk about other people in order to either restore or give you a permanent sense of yourself.*

Do you ever get afraid? If you will refuse to go along with the fear that you feel, consciously refuse to do its bidding when it directs you how to protect yourself from the enemy it has projected on to the screen of your mind, you will become conscious of *the fear* as the psychic intruder, the intimate enemy, that it really is. This new, higher self-awareness is the seed of a rebellion within yourself that God wants you to stage. He *will give you* what you need at *that* point to set you free from the fear, or whatever that inner tyrant may be, that's overshadowing you.

Are you beginning to understand how these new inner actions are indeed new *prayers?* As you are able to see them for the invitation that they are—for God to take your side—then you'll also start to see how you can extend this conscious invitation all the time and everywhere you go. One more example will show you that this is true.

Don't you want the last word in any disagreement, regardless of its seeming importance, even if you don't speak it out loud, but only utter it in the smoldering depths of your mind? You know exactly what I'm taking about! If *you* don't have that last word . . . surely you're going to die!

Consciously giving up the last word is a secret prayer because the you that wants the last word isn't really you at all—it's that dark spirit of one-upmanship, that dark spirit of combativeness. When you say "I" to it, it's the same as giving your whole life to it. But when you don't express it for the first time, you'll become conscious of its presence in you and you will realize its presence *is a punishment*, not some power that it passes itself off as being while you're identified with it.

Look at all the new ways in which you're learning to pray. And incidentally, talk about praying in secret! No one will know what you're doing. You won't even know what you're doing for a long time! That's the truth. And that's all right. You'll hear inside of you other visitors telling you, "If you don't express this you're going to explode!" Don't listen to them. Listen instead to Truth's instructions in any of these inner situations. Here it is: Truth says to go ahead and dare that visitor to do *everything* it can do to you, including taking your life if that's what it wants! You stand upon the Ground of Truth. You watch yourself. Don't push anything away—or down—and don't give yourself up to what wants your life. To change the metaphor, you remain with God. You remain with what is eternal, what is timeless. You remain within what is *not* the state. Oh, what a work, what an activity. Oh, what a divine way to spend your day!

Allow me to add one last note to this study in learning to truly possess yourself. It's very important for your inner development to come up with your own new prayers-in-action based upon what you see about yourself. Every person attracts certain types of inner visitors, and no single prayer-in-action works for every person. Your spiritual life requires you to learn a spiritual craft of a sort—a skill borne from self-observation. So take the time needed to look into your own life. See where it is that you are like what you are because of what you are allowing within you. Start this very moment to become conscious of all inner states. Your consciousness of them is the request for that Life which is not dominated by them, which is the same as requesting that God let you live within Him. This request he always answers.

Special Lessons for Self-Study

Our life experience is a direct reflection of our spiritual level in life, and our spiritual life-level is determined by what we are aware of within ourselves. Since there's no end to the levels of self-awareness, this means we secretly possess an infinite capacity for consciously elevating our life experience.

The person who does not know himself, and who accepts what his life is like without self-knowledge, receives from life both what the absence of that self-knowledge requests and what it permits.

As it becomes clear to you that your prayers are indeed being answered microsecond to microsecond, you will want more than anything else *to be* something different.

Not expressing the negative state is the same as revealing the self that is not it.

Daring any dark state to do its worst to you is the same as asking God to defend you.

We loosely talk of Self-realization, for lack of a better term. But how can one realize that which alone is real? All we need to do is to give up our habit of regarding as real that which is unreal. All religious practices are meant solely to help us do this.

—RAMANA MAHARSHI

five

In humility is the greatest freedom. As long as you have to defend the imaginary self that you think is important you lose your peace of heart. As soon as you compare that shadow with the shadows of other people, you lose all joy because you have begun to trade in unrealities, and there is no joy in things that do not exist.

—THOMAS MERTON

Find Lasting Self-Renewal in Self-Release

There's a quotation of Ralph Waldo Emerson's that speaks volumes more than the few dozen words used in its telling. Which is why, even after having known it for a long time and being able to recite it by heart, I am still highly attracted to its secret communication. Perhaps you will also feel it drawing upon something deep within you. It says:

83

Is not prayer a study of truth, a sally of the soul
into the unfound infinite?

And then it finishes this thought with a last line that
adds yet another measure of mystery to it, enhancing further, for me, its attraction.

No man, no woman, ever prayed heartily without
learning something.

What about you? When you think of prayer, do you
consider it as a journey into what is true, not as merely an
intellectual pursuit or ideal, but as a deliberate act that delivers you up and into something unfound *within* the
Truth?

Prayer is a study
of truth.

What form of "hearty prayer" teaches the
one who prays *not* about those weary and
worn closed boundaries of the known, but
delivers the prayer beyond these restrictions
of finite life into the realm of the Infinite? What study of
truth does this? What manner of prayer is it that reaches
"into the unfound infinite," and in the same instant teaches
the soul what its heart has longed to know?

Do you feel this tug in your heart to transcend yourself,
to be free to journey into a place of infinite renewal? To discover what is unfound within and therein to know its Secret
Founder? Good! Because what pulls on you from within in
this way is trying to get you *to let go of yourself.* And the secret of this self-release is found only in self-study whose
fruit is the Truth that sets us free. Said slightly differently, to
know ourselves is to know the need for prayer; and the

heart that knows *this* need, that longs to be released and renewed, is teacher, teaching, and the taught.

On the small wooden deck just outside my office, where I study and do my writing, sits a big terra-cotta pot that is home for a strange mixture of green onions and strawberries. This odd-shaped urn is a catch-all, something that my wife wasn't too fond of and so it got deposited on my deck to be watered. I've brought you into my home life for this brief moment for this reason:

If I don't water that planter almost daily during the dog days of summer, those poor plants rooted in it start looking like I do after a hard day working outside in the heat—weary and wilted! Nothing in that planter can even stand up anymore, and the color of life itself seems to have seeped out of the leaves. All the plants are collapsed over the edge of the pot and I'm sure they're speaking in faint whispers: "If we don't get some water *now*, you're going to have an empty pot on your hands!"

Everyone knows what happens to plants when we fail to water them. Then you pour water on them, and within two or three hours their life returns—the leaves stand up again, looking healthy as can be. So the plant goes from being in this condition: "Please help me or I'm going die" (if you could hear its cries) to, "Happy days are here again!" The new watering has completely refreshed its life, and that's a very apt metaphor for the miracle of what our own spiritual life is intended to be like.

For the majority of us, what we consider being renewed has nothing to do with what is real renewal. Mostly what we feel as renewal is when some idea or a hope that we have gets fulfilled, filling us in turn with a sense of excitement; and then, in that feeling of being full of ourselves, comes a certain kind of pleasure that we take as being the same as self-renewal in this life. But there's a problem with this sense of renewal, isn't there? As all of us know too well, there is a point in our lives when we even stop looking for that kind of joy because we understand that as fast as it pours in, it pours out! In fact, no matter how much the world pours into us that way—with good financial fortune or whatever it is—no matter how much we seem to come into, there remains an emptiness. Here's the reason behind this truth.

Our souls are not enlarged through circumstance. As a matter of fact, contrary to being enlarged by those circumstantial experiences that grant us a temporary sense of self-renewal, we're more often than not unconsciously limited by them. The more you hold on to what are obviously conditional aspects of this life—for that sense of yourself of being "new" or "going forward"—the more afraid you are that you're going to lose

Our souls are not enlarged through circumstance.

it. So in this there's no real renewal in it at all. The little-understood secret of life is that everything we *add* to our cup to make ourselves greater becomes the very thing that makes us less. But there it is.

The example of the old earthen pot and its thirsty little plants provides us with a wonderful example of how it is possible to see the deeply spiritual in life's simplest things; to find what I call the Celestial in the common. One moment, the drought-stricken plant can barely draw a breath; and then, in comes the life-giving water and it's restored, renewed.

Water has been used as a symbol for life-restoring truth since the beginning of time. To be washed clean and have our thirst quenched are not two different moments. They are one motion, the same act. We're intended to have the understanding and *to experience this kind of renewal* that only the Truth can pour into us. That's why it's so vital for our continuing development to not only be willing to see the truth of the following, but to work to understand the actual inner dynamics that keep us from experiencing real self-renewal.

In those times when we're busy dreaming up the next plan, the next love, the next thrill—whatever that may be— aren't we really looking for a way to renew ourselves? And isn't the vehicle that delivers this longed-for feeling always some sort of a mental image? A self-created picture that pleases us just to gaze upon it on the screen of our mind? Are you able to see the way this works within you? Consider when you think: I need a feeling of something to spice up my life, so I'm going to go on a trip, buy myself that special something, or find a new relationship. This means that in your mind, there is now a picture of pleasure or happiness-to-come. In that same moment, this new pleasurable image is filled with that new pleasure you've just pictured. *But it's just a picture.* Let's look deeper.

Suppose you dress up in the new clothes, take the trip, make that purchase, or mastermind that next new deal.

Then what? You no more get into these things than they get themselves into you. There's no end to it. Even before you're back from that dream vacation you have to plan a "better" trip. Then you have to have more clothes, better this, more of whatever, and instead of finding the freedom naturally attending real renewal, you find you've become the prisoner of your own inventions! But it should also be said that these facts don't imply we shouldn't enjoy what is natural physical renewal. There's nothing wrong with wanting to step out of the world of hum-drum routine work. Actually, it's necessary. After all, if you work hard at home, or at work, you *should* get outside the confines of that realm and go enjoy nature, or read a book, or listen to music. To relax in this way is to live from different parts of yourself that allow those tired parts to renew themselves. But if our wish is to become new men and women, to find our place in the "unfound infinite," then the spiritual renewal required for this inner transformation cannot be found along the known lines of our physical plane.

Which brings us to the first "catch." We're looking to our own best ideas, to those well-preserved images from our own past experiences, *which are all a part of the physical realm,* to guide us to something New. But the word *new* itself means "never having been before; the first of, etc." Think about it.

If something is truly new this means *nothing was before it.* However, our present knowledge of life and self doesn't understand *this kind* of "new." For us, "new" is how we look after dieting or plastic surgery; the next series in the line of cars we'd like to drive; the next revelation about some movie star's unhappy life, or whatever it may be. If this sounds shallow, it is. Our spiritual lives have been so starved of reality's nourishing inflow that almost all of what we now think of as being "new" is little more than an unconscious continuation of some reconfigured past experience.

Do try to see the truth of this—that when you think of finding something *new*, you don't think about something that *has never been before*. What you're looking for, unconsciously, is that familiar sense of self-renewal that comes with finding something similar to what you already knew, even though it didn't fulfill you the last time you embraced its kissing cousin. Speaking of which, to use just one example, look at the merry-go-round of personal relationships everyone rides. With each go-round, the hope is that "this time" it will be different. Even if you do manage to ride a horse of a different color, in no time at all it loses its bright luster and leaves you feeling like you need another newer, shinier one!

Stop thinking in terms of continuity; begin working toward a discontinuity.

Our investigation has brought us to a very important point that will prove itself worth your extra study: For real Newness to come into your life, you must learn to stop thinking in terms of a continuity and begin working consciously toward *discontinuity*. The next paragraph will help shed some light on this unusual idea.

So far we've learned in this chapter that we unconsciously tend to search along the lines of some existing continuity.

In other words, that we always look at *what once was* in our lives in order to picture *what might be*. But now we can begin to understand that before something genuinely new can appear in our lives something old must pass. There must be a *discontinuation*. But perhaps you're wondering: a discontinuity of what? There must be discontinuity of "I," of our familiar sense of self. Still more to the point of this study, there must be a discontinuity of that sense of "I" from which we look out into our world in order to find something that we believe will renew us.

For many reasons about to be revealed, let's say there are two basic kinds of prayer. The first kind of prayer we've just been examining—the one most commonly understood and practiced—is when you are asking for what you want; when you are temporarily filled with—and renewed by—both the self making that request and the anticipation of what is requested. This is the only kind of prayer that most men and women ever know; when someone asks *from himself* for something *for himself*. Examples of this kind of prayer are as easy to produce as listening to your own thoughts tell you why you're unhappy with your life. "Please send me some money." "Please straighten out my problem." "Please arrange a happy ending for me." In this kind of prayer, the person praying knows what he or she wants, as well as how that prayer ought to be happily answered.

Ask God to be in charge of your life without telling how.

But there is another kind of prayer. A special form of invocation exists that is virtually unknown in these days of ever-increasing ignorance of ourselves. This secret prayer is when you ask God to be in charge of your life without telling how. This powerful kind of prayer—and praying— develops within you in definite stages, but it begins with learning to ask the Almighty to help to you help yourself see the truth about your life, even while knowing it will probably reveal something about yourself that you don't want to see. For instance, you might say silently in your heart, "Please, Almighty . . . show me what I need to see about myself." Or perhaps, "Blessed Mother . . . I'm so weary with all that I know to ask for. Please teach me, whatever the cost, to learn how to ask for something new."

Briefly summarizing the difference between these two distinct types of prayer, the first one is where *you* are in charge of what you think you must have to be happy. Here you are trying to light your own way, struggling daily to straighten out the darkened and crooked places in your life that lie both ahead of and behind you.

The second kind of prayer is the one critical for real self-renewal. With this prayer you ask God to be in charge of your life, to give you *not what you think you want*, but what *He knows you need* in order to enlarge your relationship with Him. In this prayer you're not looking for anything for yourself outside of asking God to remove the veils from your eyes.

The whole of your new wish, this change in how you want to consciously change the way you've been approaching your life, is your agreement to discontinue yourself. This new willingness on your part for God's will to supplant your own invites His Life to pour into yours. In comes the water that renews your life. You find yourself more alive than when you were struggling to give yourself the life you hoped for. Perhaps better said, you find yourself newly alive, but the "you" that is brought to life when God is in charge interiorly isn't you—and yet it is. Words for how one can both *be*—and at the same time *have no being* apart from the Almighty—have been the musings of poets and saints down through the ages. All agree that the impossible, once described, becomes impoverished by its own description. Still, the words of Mme. Jeanne Guyan are rich with an unspoken invitation to the spiritually hungry heart: "The boundless sea has absorbed the river and its limited waters. Now the river shares in all the sea has. The sea carries the river along; the river cannot carry itself along. The river has become one with the sea. No, the river does not have all the qualities of the sea, but it is, nonetheless, in the sea."

Now, how do we bring about this extraordinary exchange? First, it's essential for you to have a new order of self-knowledge. This elevated understanding is borne out of a higher awareness of your present self. A short spiritual riddle will help take us up the next step in this new self-study.

Name that mysterious element, which when brought into these five following everyday conditions, actually serves to ruin them. Got it? Let's see how sharp you are!

> *Condition one:* She turns to him at the restaurant saying she needs him to give her a little more space to discover herself. In "it" rushes and ruins the moment.

Condition two: He picks up the paper and "it" pops out between the lines of the headlines that announce a new financial plan for the large corporation that employs him.

Do you know what "it" is yet? Remember, we're trying to name that mysterious element that when brought into these five totally different conditions ruins each of them.

Condition three: His partner tells him that all their good work looks like it's about to pay off and in that moment, out "it" spills, first dampening the moment and then spoiling it.

Condition four: She says at long last: "I need you" to someone she's been slowly getting involved with, and in the next heartbeat "it" turns against her.

Are you getting any closer to solving the riddle? Here's the last clue. In the fifth and final condition your boss tells you to do some task the way he or she prefers, and out "it" leaps.

Won't you agree that these are pretty different conditions for the same thing to appear in and to cause the same results? Some happy, some not. Some stressful, some not. Can you name this mysterious element?

If you said the word "I," congratulations are in order, but most likely you weren't able to solve this spiritual riddle. For good reason, too. The last thing that any of us want to know about ourselves is that our usual "I" is, in fact, the secret culprit stepping in and wrecking our life experience, bringing unnecessary conflict into even simple moments. This most intimate of enemies even has command over our mouths! Have any of you ever had your mouth taken over by some overpowering "I," and then later you said, "I don't know why I said that!" As a still deeper lesson in humility, have you noticed how—after you've put your foot

The usual "I" is the secret culprit wrecking our life experience.

in your own mouth—*then* you believe that the "I" that pops in to explain the "I" that took your mouth over is the real you? The real self that knows better and is overall in charge of all the other "I"s? Sorry! No such luck!

Let me tell you about a fascinating experience of mine that will give us both necessary new knowledge about the invisible nature of this "I" as well as how, in the light of what we learn, our prayer life can help us begin making the connection to That alone with the power to grant lasting self-renewal.

The purpose these inner-life studies—and that of my upcoming short true story—is to reveal our need for a whole, new "I." This real "I"—if you happen to be Christocentrically oriented—is the Christ: the one Real "I" in all men and all women, an ever-renewing "I." Not coincidentally, this same idea of awakening to one's True Self is described in one fashion or another as both the purpose and the heart of every major religion.

Consider for a moment that everybody in the world has a sense of "I." The problem is that your prevailing sense of "I" in any given moment is often quite different from mine, and when we're in agreement we get along great. But when your "I" goes against my "I," when you've got an "I" that says, "*This* is God" and my "I" that says, "No. *This* is God," these two "I"s will go at it, hating one another over who knows the most about the one source of Love—all the while never even noticing the monstrous contradiction in which they are stranded. How can such a condition occur? The personal experience I promised to tell will help explain how so much unconscious conflict and pain stays in place.

I once lived in a little house whose many windows opened by sliding from side to side. Each one had a small, thin locking latch that slid up and down on the window's side and was designed to catch into a slot on the frame. So, if you wanted to open any window you had to pull the latch up and then slide the window over.

Even during the hottest days of summer, I rarely would run my in-the-wall air-conditioner because of the noise it made and its high electric cost. So every night before I'd go to bed, I'd have this ritual where I went around opening every single window in the house, and come the next morning, I'd slide all the windows closed because the house had cooled down and closing them helps keep the coolness in. But because I'm sliding open and closed these windows every night and morning, I finally just scotch-taped their little lock-latches up. Now, if you have this picture in mind, I'll go on with the story.

One August morning, about five o'clock or so and still dark outside, I was up and sitting in my small living room, just enjoying the deep quiet the country life affords, especially in those hours before sunrise. My attention was mine and my eyes were closed. A great silence attended me.

Then, all of a sudden, a piece of scotch tape holding up the little locking latch on one of the nearby windows gave way, and that little latch slid down and it went "click." But something else clicked in that moment as well! In that split second something of a very unusual order took place within me. A tremendous secret was revealed about the hidden workings of my own psychology, a discovery that should help to greatly energize your inner wish—and your prayer life—to discontinue "I."

However, the key here, and where our story will take us as it continues, is that you can't work to discontinue your usual sense of "I" until you start to understand that your usual sense of "I" isn't at all *who you really are*. You can't even begin to think about sacrificing who you think you are until you have the knowledge and the inner vision that shows you that the "you" that is presently, literally, living out your life for you *is not you*. Now for the rest of the story. Your patience in trying to understand the following sequence of inner and outer events will be rewarded ... so do persist!

When that little latch on my living room window went down and clicked, at the split second that it clicked, it was enough of an unexpected noise that it made my body jump. So, to describe this moment of being startled, I would have to say that "I" jumped a little bit. But here's where it gets interesting. You see it was another "I" that actually heard and registered the noise of the click. Let me explain.

That morning, aided by the deep silence there with me, I could see the "I" that jumped first. This was my body being active in a pure physical reaction to an unknown sound. Then I could see that I heard that which had just made me jump. In other words, after I was startled, I became conscious of the click sound that caused it. So, to lay out the sequence of events that morning first "I" jumped, then "I" heard, and finally "I" knew what that sound was I had just heard. What I'm working to describe to you, and what I hope you glean from this account, is that in the space of one heartbeat there appeared within me at least three different "I"s. One that moved, one that heard, and then one that knew why it jumped and what it heard that made it do that. Here's the point: the "I" that knew all of this was the last to come!

Your usual sense of "I" isn't at all who you really are.

Look, have you ever been suddenly scared by something? So scared that you jumped? And when you jumped, then you realized you were so scared that you acted before you even knew what had scared you? This is a common instinctive condition in human beings commonly thought of as self-preservation. What I'm pointing out here is that your sudden movement had nothing to do with any "self-knowing" at all, and that the part of you that "heard" the disturbing sound—that "I"—is nothing but a link, a kind of psychic connecting point between the unfolding physical world and the interior world of conditioned thought and feeling. That's all this or any similarly produced sense of "I"

is. It's an interpreter that performs its duty based upon past personal knowledge. We can prove this discovery.

Suppose for a moment that someone else was in the room with me that morning, eyes closed as were mine, enjoying the silence. Now imagine that this person has no idea what that metallic "click" was, but that he believed that before angels talk, they make a short, metallic click-like sound. At that moment this person in the room with me would say, "I heard an angel!" because that "I" would be explaining the experience to him through the content of his knowledge. But is that "I" that explains the content of the experience a real "I"? No! And the next insight is a vital one, so try to see all of its immense implications: the moment that the event changes, the "I" changes. The sliding window lock-latch created a noise that produced an "I," but that "I" is just a product of past knowledge. It's not who you *really* are any more than an encyclopedia is wise in and of itself.

The moment that the event changes, the "I" changes.

How can we use the valuable insights gained from this true story? Start by seeing that your own thoughts make "click" sounds inside of you. The events don't have to be just windows closing, or things dropping, or doors slamming. The event can be a thought that passes through your mind. And when it does it makes a "click," it brings what feels like a "knowing" self to the forefront of your window of consciousness. And then out of that appearance comes another "I" that seemingly continues the whole experience by explaining to you what the first "I" saw. On and on it goes.

These familiar feelings of "I" are not you. They belong to your name, to who *you've been*, to the whole psychological package that you know as your present "self." It is critical for your spiritual growth to start understanding that from this package and within its given lineage of "I"s no real renewal can occur. This discovery is the secret meaning behind Christ's edict that "the first shall be last and the last shall be first."

This new knowledge reveals "for those who have eyes to see" that real prayer, the soul-transforming kind, goes and grows hand in hand with real self-discovery. It begins as you inwardly, unmistakably, realize that in order for you to be renewed your prayer must include the understanding for the necessity of consciously discontinuing yourself. There is ample proof for this position.

Do you recall that most famous moment in Christ's life framed by this eternal passage of perfect self surrender? "Not my will but Thy will be done." Isn't that a discontinuity of "I"? This wish for discontinuity of self cannot be based upon desire, because desire itself is the continuity of "I." So this wise and new action must be based upon *insight*. Yes. The Truth does set you free. And the reason the Truth sets you free is because it alone reveals that what you are held captive by has no reality outside of your wish to continue as you.

The falling out of love with yourself begins with seeing that the "you" that's in love with you is just as unreal as the "you" that it loves! That your life is the way it is because you are living from a series of small "I"s which care nothing for you because these false selves are themselves, in truth, noth-ings. As you start to see that, you start giving up "I." You start letting "I" go. That's prayer, because it is self-disconti-nuity; a conscious act of self-suspension arising from a new wish for something new to occur; an act of Higher under-standing borne from knowing that being wrapped up in the old can only produce more of the old.

If you try to establish a relationship with God based on your ideas of God, and on your ideas of you, you will get what you asked for, but you won't be renewed. It'll be the renewal that you have to renew again and again. When God is in charge of your life, in your interior world, new-ness just pours in. Make no mistake about this: when these waters are being poured in *you know* something is pouring in. Perhaps best of all, you also know that what it is pouring into isn't the "you" that you thought it would pour into. God can only pour what is Himself into Himself. And be-cause you have worked to discontinue yourself, you're the lucky one having that experience. Everything Good follows this. Do your inner work, people. Do your inner work.

Special Lessons for Self-Study

If you try to establish a relationship with God based
solely on your present ideas of Him, you'll most
likely receive what *this level of self* has requested,
but *you* won't be renewed.

Everything that we add to our cup to make ourselves
greater becomes the very thing that makes us less.

Real prayer begins when you start to understand that
in order for you to be renewed, that prayer must
include the understanding for the need to
consciously discontinue yourself.

Truth sets you free because only through its eyes can you
see that what you are held captive by has no reality
outside of your wish to continue as you.

Falling out of love with yourself begins with seeing
that the "you" that is in love with you is just as
unreal as the you that it loves.

Mark how to know yourself. To know himself a
man must ever be on the watch over himself,
holding his outer faculties. This discipline must be
continued until he reaches a state of consciousness . . . .
The object is to reach a state of consciousness—a
new state of oneself. It is to reach now, where one
is present to oneself. What I say unto you I say
unto all, "be awake."

—Meister Eckhart

six

L et us love not with words or tongue, but with action and in Truth.

—NEW TESTAMENT

Seven Silent Prayers that Turn Your Life Around

Great spiritual secrets do exist and they are *not* hidden from sight. Far from it. These truths are self-evident. But if these timeless, reality-based facts of life are right before our eyes, why do they seem so elusive? There is a reason. To understand it we need only call upon our own past personal experience.

Have you ever tried saying something truthful to someone you care about? Something that everyone else sees about his or her character, but that they don't? You fill in the blanks. Perhaps he's been hurting himself with some form of self-defeating behavior, or she just can't stop being cruel to her friends or loved ones, and so you try to intervene in some way? If you've ever tried, even at the simplest level, to tell someone a potentially life-healing truth, you also know it doesn't necessarily mean that person will *understand* it. Why not? He can't, or she won't, *see* what is true. And here we uncover one of these great secrets that is right before all of us, but seen by only the willing.

In the spiritual realm, *seeing* is understanding. Perhaps this is why Christ often said that the secrets he spoke of were visible only to those who "had eyes to see." There are many reasons why we can't see what is right in front of us. The last chapter's discussion about how we live from mistaken "I"s gives us a chance to play on this word.

Real spiritual studies are about earning the right to share in the Secret of the Universe.

And here is another secret in plain sight. As we've been learning from these new self-studies, our "I"s cannot always see, yet there are still other reasons the Great Secrets of Life must sadly remain secrets even though they are in plain sight. Perhaps the principal reason is best explained by another universal truth, one that seems to be increasingly invisible these days: *you cannot have something that you haven't earned.* Real spiritual studies and the inner work they point to are about *earning* the right to share in the Secret of the

Universe: to take *conscious* part in the life of God; to become real, new, and eternal.

The following four sentences are examples of spiritual secrets in plain sight. Within these four insights—also hidden
right before our eyes—is more of the new understanding
we need to go further with our wish to become genuinely
new men and women. Here we go:

> You cannot receive anything more from life
> than the way you think toward it.
>
> You cannot think towards life other than
> the way in which you see it.
>
> You cannot see life other than through
> the ideas you have about it. So . . .
>
> To change what you receive from life, you must
> have a new perception of it, beginning with
> new ideas about it.

Are you able to see and follow the logic? Please don't
gloss over this section, regardless of what may be your
temporary resistance to working through such mental for-
mulations. Remember, you must earn the right *to see*. This
doesn't mean you must understand what you don't, only
that you be willing to try and then to experience what are
your own best efforts. I assure you if you'll do your part,
the Truth will take care of the rest. This is another great
secret! Now let's keep moving ahead. The explanations
that follow will help clear up any remaining confusion
you may have about these new ideas.

You cannot receive anything more from life than the way you think toward it. How evident is that? What do you receive from life? What happens to you when you walk into the office or pick up the phone? What happens when you go to the market or when you do your banking business; when you're talking to other people? You are in a constant state of reception, aren't you? And what

We pursue what we do because of the way we see it.

you're receiving, every split second, is intimately connected to, dependent upon, the way you think toward the life that you're meeting. Here's proof:

Take any two people and have them meet the same challenging life event. One person thinks about it without complaint or feeling defeated by it, and the other person meets it only to be overcome with self-doubt, anxiety, and worry. The first person rises above this moment while the second one is washed away by it. This shows that one man's experience of the identical event is totally different from the other man's, which proves that each receives from life the way he thinks toward the life he meets. Is this clear to you? Let's continue.

You cannot think toward life other than the way you see it. Can you see that the choices that you make every single day are based upon the way you look at life? Why does one man or one woman spend his or her life pursuing one path, and another person pursuing a different path? It's because this person sees life in a certain way that says to him, "*This* is what's valuable," and the other person sees life in a way that says to her, "No, *this* is what's valuable." One person pursues money, one person pursues a relationship, one person pursues a life of Truth, perhaps. The reason that we pursue what we do is because of the way we see it.

You cannot see life other than through your ideas about it. This person pursues what he or she does because of the ideas they have about life. This man thinks to himself, "Unless I have lots of good possessions, I'm no one." She thinks, "Unless someone loves me, I mean nothing." Everyone lives within, and responds to, life from a certain psycho-spiritual conditioning where they see life through their ideas about it. Think this realization through so that the next and final idea in this short study can deliver its intended lesson.

To change what you receive from life, you must have a new perception of it that begins with new ideas about it. You can't begin receiving anything truly new from this life as long as you continue to see it as you presently do, which is through your present ideas about it. This is so important. Our perception now—the way we tend to see ourselves—is determined largely by one particular idea we have about this life of ours. We believe life comes to us from outside of us, meaning that as you and I see life it seems to originate "out there" and then comes toward us, eventually entering into our experience. This is our present perception. This finding reveals that we live from a psychic nature that is very passive; a certain level of consciousness where the way in which we know ourselves, for the most part, depends on what our senses and reactions have perceived as being outside of us. Now, while holding these last ideas in mind, consider this passage from the New Testament:

John the Baptist, a man dedicated to preparing the way for the messiah promised in the Old Testament, taught that any person who wanted to experience real life should "repent, repent." This was followed by his admonition that "the Kingdom of Heaven is at hand." Are you familiar with the passage?

In the ancient Aramaic, the language used in that region of the world during Christ's time, the word *repent* did not have the negative connotation it carries today. It *never* meant that you were necessarily an "evil" person. Today the idea of repenting is usually filled with a painful subtext of self-recrimination, isn't it? But back then the word "repent" did not suggest that you should suffer over your past. The actual translation of *repent*, or as close as we can come using modern English, was a very *present*-oriented word meaning *to turn around.* To "repent" was a spiritual instruction urging the individual to turn in another direction. In essence what John was really saying is, "Turn yourself around. The Kingdom is here . . . *now!*"

At the beginning of this study, we reached an understanding that the course, quality, and even the content of our lives is determined by the way in which we *see* ourselves; that our present perception of life, and self, is all locked up in largely unconscious considerations such as how much we think we have, what's to become of what was or what may be, what we think people are thinking about us and its impact, and on it goes. So that living from this view of life, virtually everything *outside* of us determines the quality of our lives.

If we are secret captives of this outer circle where our experience of life is shaped by our ideas about it, and these same ideas are themselves but a part of life's hidden merry-go-round going nowhere soul satisfying, then the only hope we have of getting off of it begins with what? New ideas!

Unless we have new ideas to see our world through, we'll just keep receiving that life we already know through the ideas that we presently live from. In other words, we'll keep receiving what living at this life level yields in return. It's vital for us to expose this invisible inner circle and to make its existence as

Turn yourself around. The Kingdom is here . . . now!

clear as possible. Here's why: If we can see that within this circle of self there's no way out taking the known direction our present ideas confirm—if we can see we're all wrapped up in our ideas, and that these ideas of ours are produced by our past experiences loaded and reloaded back into us through conditioned reactions to events—then the question of how to turn around in life takes on sudden and new meaning. But turn around to what? This brings us to a question whose answer will tell us more about this needed new direction in which we must learn to turn.

When you meet someone, where does that meeting take place? For instance, say you walk down the street and someone walks up and greets you. You say, "I met them on Sixth Street." Of course that's accurate, but it misses the mark in this study because we're aiming higher. The actual physical location where you're with another person, whether you walk into someone's office or home, is only one dimension of your meeting place. A lesser one at that. Where you *really* meet everyone *is within what you are.* Please, think about this secret until it's evident to you. The next example should prove helpful.

A friend enters your kitchen, or a fellow employee walks into your office. Sure, you've met there in a certain spot, but the real meeting place, the one that counts, is within what you are. A moment's consideration proves the point. Have you ever been a nicer person on one day than on another? Of course you have. Inwardly, when you're feeling good about life, you meet that person—or any person—in a *better* place. You can put up with almost anyone when you meet them within yourself in a nice place, can't you? But when you're in a bad place inwardly, God help anyone that walks in to meet you because you will meet them *within* what you are. So can you understand that whatever it is that you meet, no matter where you meet it, no matter what you're doing, you meet him, her, it, within what you are and no place else? If you've understood this great secret, then you're ready for another one.

Where you meet everyone is within what you are.

When you, as God wills it, come to know Him, *where* will you meet His Life? You will meet that Supreme Being *within* yourself. You can't meet anything in life outside of what we'll call your self. There is no other place. Let this secret sink in. "Ah. I meet everyone within what I am. I will also meet God within what I am. When I'm standing in the Kingdom of Heaven, when I attain Nirvana, when the Buddha Nature reveals itself, (name it as you please), I'll be standing within what 'I Am' because in reality there is no other place."

This great secret initiates you into yet another powerful lesson. It points out that if you continue living as you presently are, as an outer-oriented person, you will be doomed to re-create your life the way it has always been. This recurrence is reincarnation of self by the self. Only as it cycles back through itself this life tends to descend and get worse because the false self gets smaller as it psychically circles back through itself. The instruction for how to break out of this circle of self is partially revealed in the discovery of this circle's existence and its inherent limitations. The good news is that there *is* another you, another Life where your experience of yourself is completely different because you've turned around. You've escaped the circle of self by learning to face in a whole new direction.

Now, just for fun, and because it will help make everything we've just studied clearer for you, please finish reading this paragraph and then set the book down while you follow these simple instructions. Wherever you may be as you're reading this book, set it down and physically turn yourself around so that you'll be looking in the opposite direction. When you do this, you'll see your actions have placed you in an entirely different relationship with your surroundings. Please do this now and then resume reading.

The point of this short exercise in awareness is to reveal that at least one aspect of relationship always has to do with the direction you're facing. Until you understand what it means to turn around, even in the most physical sense of the words, you can't have that new relationship that turning around naturally, effortlessly, produces.

Prayer is intended to be deliberate, conscious inner work to help you turn your life around. What's the new direction? *Inward.* We know how we are now. This whole chapter has been one lesson after another about what is clearly our *outwardly* directed life. The secret I'm trying to tell you is that there are no new ideas that you are going to receive from the self that is looking where it is looking. The only world it knows doesn't have new ideas. Something truly new can happen to you only within the ever-becoming inner world, and prayer is intended to help you to realize both this eternal Newness within yourself as well as to reveal yet another great secret: This newness is your True Self.

With all of this in mind, we learned in chapter 5 that there were two basic kinds of prayers and of prayer. One type of prayer wants to be in charge of their spiritual life the way they dream they're in command of their physical life—being active and asking for what they just know is missing from their life that would finally fulfill them *if only* God would listen. The second prayer is a person who simply asks God to be in charge of everything. In this next chapter section, we're going to look into a kind of special internal work in which there are two ways to pray.

There's a story in the New Testament about two sisters, Martha and Mary, whose meager home was being visited by Christ. Martha couldn't stop running around the house. She was everywhere—cooking this, cleaning that, endlessly busy with one thing or another to help ensure Christ's visit would be comfortable. She never stopped!

Mary, on the other hand, sat the whole time with Christ. She first washed the dust from his feet and then poured expensive oil over them. Apparently this was too much for her sister because it was then that Martha spoke out against Mary, thinking that Christ would take her side in the reprimand. "You never help me!" she cried. "Look at all I'm doing while you're just sitting there!" Of course, we don't get the whole story, but our own experience in similar moments lets us identify with both sides of these sisters bickering! Anyway, at that moment Christ spoke up, correcting Martha, saying to her something to the effect that, "Mary has the best part." What did Christ mean by this? It connects with what we've been learning.

There are two types of relationship with the Truth, with God.

In this short story we learn through Christ's words—in his brief correction of Martha's spirit towards her sister—that there are two ways to pray or, perhaps better stated, that there are two types of relationship with the Truth, with God, but that these two ways are *very* different.

The first way, Martha's way, connects with our earlier lesson about the first kind of person—the prayer who wants to be in charge of life by struggling to get from it what they imagine it will give. Martha thought Christ—representing God, Truth—would be delighted with her devotion to him; something she hoped she was expressing by running herself ragged. In short, she was trying to win Christ's favor by doing what she hoped would make a favorable impression. We all understand this behavior, and should also realize that it is the seed of resentment as evidenced each time that other person fails to notice our excellence.

The second way, Mary's way of prayer as it were, was to have no concern with what Christ might give her, but only with expressing her deep and natural spiritual love for the Light in human form now actually there in her home. Her only thought was to be as close to him as possible. It's important to point out that there was no fault with Martha's actions, only that Mary's actions were superior in that they brought her into closer relationship with the new life that Christ's life represents. We're taught in this story about two different actions that represent two different aspects of prayer. One, Martha's, is expressed outwardly; the other, Mary's, inwardly.

The specialized prayers about to be introduced are ways that you may begin working to become inwardly active in your life in a whole new way. These seven silent prayers that turn your life around are designed to help you begin this highly individualized work of turning yourself around and to consciously reorient yourself to the world awaiting you within.

The first of the seven silent prayers that turn your life around is:

Refuse to defend yourself when anyone else wrongly accuses you.

Now why is that action a prayer? What has not defending yourself got to do with prayer? You see, the way we are now, when someone accuses us of doing something wrong, the first thing we want to do is to find a way to re-establish our now-upset sense of well-being. We defend what we take as our self from what we perceive as our attacker. This action focuses our attention outside of us, not on the inner man or the inner woman, where the real weakness or misunderstanding exists. By employing this new prayer-in-action, which is to refuse to defend yourself when wrongly accused, you consciously cut yourself off from the idea-oriented outer self that will, in turn, help to make you conscious of the inner person. And never mind what you see or hear in your inner world as you work at this—all of those voices hammering at you saying, "Oh! If I don't defend myself something bad is going to happen to me." The all-important step is to reorient your attention, to become wide awake. Become a conscious witness to everything passing through your newly illuminated inner world instead of being the unconscious servant of your image-driven outer life.

Number two:

> **Deliberately dare to slow down your life**
> **when everything in you—or around you—**
> **is screaming "Rush."**

Why is this bold action a prayer? Every person knows what it feels like to be carried off by an anxious state so you decide: when some anxiety comes along and takes over your life—are you an awake inwardly centered person—or are you an unconscious outwardly driven man or woman? Which are you? That you're outwardly directed is pretty obvious. Why? Because that anxious state could not exist without your false belief that who you are—your well-being—is connected to something happening exterior to yourself. And now this mistaken idea is driving you, compelling you to get this thing fixed or that situation resolved *right now*, because once you have, you'll be back in a peaceful place. As long as you take yourself as someone who has something to lose because of your identification with any temporary exterior condition or circumstance, you will remain someone subject to every outer condition.

By deliberately slowing yourself down when everything in you seems to be screaming "Rush," you will become inwardly awake. You'll become conscious of yourself in a new way. For the first time you'll understand that these anxiety attacks have nothing to do with what didn't get done, or with what "might happen," but that their painful place dwells within a belief-packed self you're living from that has convinced you that if you don't answer the situation *it* says has caused your anxiety, you'll end up losing something valuable. This new kind of prayer-in-action changes your perception of yourself by turning your attention around to where the real problem, and the real solution, exists— *within you*. This simple but powerful prayer will help you make the transforming transition to find your life inside of you instead of forever looking for a way to fix it by struggling outside of you.

Number three:

> **Doing what you don't want to do when you don't want to do it.**

About the only time you and I really *want* to handle the things we must is when everything in us agrees that this is the time to do it; translated, this means that we're only happy doing what we must when we're going to feel the most comfortable doing it. This resistance we run into within ourselves when facing unwanted tasks is created by two sets of unconscious conditioned notions we have within ourselves as to the real nature of comfort. First that real comfort is determined by a set of exterior conditions that can be manipulated. And secondly, as part of the unconscious

On the other side of the resistance is the flow.

belief hidden in the first, if these conditions cannot be made to match our preconceived notions, then real comfort is impossible.

Of course it's nice to have things pleasant around us. But everything we're learning teaches us that finding our sense of self in anything exterior to us is the same as agreeing to lose ourselves any time these circumstances change, which they *always* do. So how does doing what you don't want to do when you don't want to do it become a prayer-in-action?

Each time you deliberately, consciously take yourself through what feels like your own resistance to doing something, here's what you'll find: *On the other side of the resistance is the flow.* Physically speaking, runners experience this new and deeper sense of self each time they challenge what their body tells them is the end of their endurance. Spiritually speaking, the self resisting any moment is a psychological body that knows itself through past experiences that have conditioned it to believe that only certain sets of circumstances will provide it with the necessary ingredients to be happy. This false self is actually threatened by anything outside of what it "knows" or "wants," which it then resists. Doing what you don't want to do is asking to unmask this false sense of self, in turn revealing that this often self-defeating sense of self is not really *you* at all! In this inner discovery you learn that real comfort, real pleasure, is in being free of that belief-loaded self whose very existence is resistance. This new freedom is an inside job.

Number four:

> **Walk away from shallow social circles where gossip, sarcasm, and one-upmanship are the coin of the realm.**

Just walk away from them. This prayer-in-action will show you—after you dare the judgment of others, or the aloneness that attends from refusing to join in society's sick circles—that the real departure you must make is from your own internal circle of thrill-seeking thoughts and false convictions. The following insights should more than prove the need for this special kind of self-quitting.

One quirk of human psychology, connected to the wrong use of imagination, is that when we don't understand the actual purpose of something, we invent one for it. A child too young to yet understand the purpose of a shoe will find ways to entertain himself with it, using it for purposes that have nothing to do with what the shoe was created for. Puppies aren't the only creatures known to chew up good leather! While there's no real problem with this kind of behavior in children, it's a different story for adults.

When men and women fail to discover the true purpose of their lives, their invented ones can often be cruel. One small example of this can be seen in our unconscious treatment of one another in various business or social settings where, in an attempt to be seen by others as being "better" than some contemporary, we may unknowingly use sarcasm to cut someone down to make us seem taller. This misunderstanding of life's purpose is secretly the same as self-ignorance. Our state of spiritual sleep actually perpetuates this unconscious assumption that winning friends and overcoming enemies is the purpose of our being because this outer struggle lends us such a strong sense of self.

We must work to turn away from any social situation where false purposes mask secret punishments, as well as from that false sense of self that seeks itself indiscriminately in these strained settings. Being willing to be alone—when necessary—is a prayer-in-action. Your willingness to walk away from this level of yourself is the same as inviting Truth to provide you with a new one, one which is already content because it is a living expression of Life's true purpose.

Number five:

Allow that uncomfortable silence to remain unfilled in that embarrassing moment.

When you're with another person, or in a group of people perhaps around a dinner table, have you ever noticed in those most unexpected moments when a sudden and uncomfortable silence pours in, you feel compelled to fill it with something? You think *anything* would feel better than that temporary nothing now demanding your attention and everyone else's attention. What is it within you that wants to rush and fill it in? Among other unconscious and self-compromising ideas is the belief that unless you do it—or someone does—that the ensuing moment of unfilled space is somehow a formal indictment of social unsuitability! In other words, this silent spot, if left unanswered, will prove that you're not that clever, all-knowing conversationalist you hope others see you as being. Just for the record, everyone involved feels this same brief attack of personal panic.

But for us the lesson in moments such as these is to come awake to ourselves and therein to see that this perceived moment of terrible emptiness feels like a pain. In other words, pressure makes you jump in. Don't jump in. *Turn around instead.* Learn to watch these moments and to use them to be in touch with the inner man, the inner woman, whose True Nature doesn't fear anything, let alone a moment of silence! Working to put yourself in touch with your own fearless, silent Self will change your relationship with yourself and life. As we'll get to later, this turning to the silence instead of away from it will allow you to move into a different kind of prayer.

Number six:

Give up the last word to someone else who's obviously glad to take it.

This prayer-in-action connects with the earlier lesson found in not defending yourself before false accusers. Only the painful and unconscious idea that not having the last word is the same as losing yourself can compel you to verbally fight with anyone in this way. Choose instead to consciously drop this losing war of words and watch how inner and outer worlds part by themselves, leaving you, at last, with the choice of where you will live.

This special spiritual understanding, and the hard self-work it calls for, will help you in other areas of your inner life as well. In learning to turn and walk away from arguments in the outer world, you're slowly earning the spiritual strength you need to let go of those interior battles where any kind of fighting is secret futility. No one wins in a dark inner dialogue except for the darkness that drags you into such a struggle with yourself.

Give up the last word to someone else who's obviously glad to take it. Let that person win what is really nothing but the false perception that he or she is a winner. Winning illusions isn't worth losing yourself. Let the world outside of you have all of its temporary conquests while you secretly claim the internal victory that wins something eternal.

The last of the seven silent prayers is:

Purposely create difficult tasks for yourself that heighten your inner awareness.

It's possible to produce for yourself—through conscious efforts—moments in which you are much more inward than outward. That's the point. You have to find your own ways in the various opportunities that life affords as you go through it, but as one example, try doing something you're sure is beyond your ability or that would drive you "nuts" if you went into it. Perhaps for a short and safe period of time while working at some task you might agree to tax yourself beyond your normally accepted tolerances of physical discomfort. Notice how much more aware you are of yourself at these moments when you've agreed by your actions to witness yourself. Or, within the limitations of what is safe and prudent, deliberately drive your car slower than the flow of thoughts within urging you to speed up. There's nothing like going against what "you" want in the moment to help keep you awake in that moment.

The key to these seven prayers-in-action is to use the events in your life to turn around and become an inner-oriented man or woman. And here's the real reason you should be willing to make these seeming sacrifices of what you take to be your self: Inward is where upward begins.

We've been discussing the necessity for turning ourselves around, to start looking in a new direction. One reason this idea appeals to us is because at least part of us realizes that what we want—what we need to become new—rests somewhere above our present understanding. That's pretty clear, isn't it? Natural too. What I want is Higher than I am. But what does this idea of something being Higher than ourselves mean? To start with, it means something more complete—something more fully integrated, more finished. When you think about what you want, and when you say to yourself that what you want is above you,

Turn around and become an inner-oriented man or woman.

you begin to realize that this upward direction can only be found one place: *inward*. Going upward within yourself must be the same as the direction in which it's possible to complete yourself. What we're talking about is finding inside of ourselves that nature that not only is capable of making the ascent, but that ascends to Itself.

We have learned that there were two "ways" to pray. In this final chapter section we've been discussing the active side as represented by how Martha behaved around Christ. Now for the other side, Mary's side. This is the side when you are by yourself, alone with the Truth, reaching out in the dark.

Let me add a brief, but very important, spiritual note here: There is no such thing as a failed prayer. What does that mean? When you eat, can you fail? No, it's impossible. Because you connect purpose with what you do. You eat to nourish yourself. You can't fail at eating. If you eat, you nourish yourself. Perhaps you've never considered this idea before, but *you pray to know yourself.*

Let's jump back for an instant to the beginning of this study when I asked you where, God Willing, you will meet God. You're going to meet this Great Life within what you are! So you pray to know what is inherently within your self. You meditate to realize your Self. These practices are not *for you to be telling yourself* what you are. That's why so many people get frustrated with prayer and meditation; they're busy trying to establish or confirm something about themselves. They're busy trying to find something instead of letting what is already there—and already perfect—instruct them about themselves.

Usually, this person sits down to silently pray or meditate and the next instant there are voices, daydreams, all manner of creatures commanding and stealing his or her attention. The brain never stops until this person cries out, "I can't stand it. I'm not getting anywhere." Yes you are! *You're meeting what you presently are*, which is what is absolutely necessary *if* you want a new you.

How else will you learn not to love that self who thinks that money, sex, food, popularity, whatever it is, is *the* solution? How else will you learn not to be associated with what you presently are, other than having a relationship with it? I know it feels as though you've "failed" at your silent search for Truth when you run into all that noise within yourself. But you have not failed. As difficult as this may be to grasp at first, you got it. To which you say, "But it's not what I wanted," meaning "What I want are my ideas about this Higher relationship." But Truth teaches and reveals through our own experience that you cannot have a Higher life until you finally learn to let go of the lower, thought-directed one.

To this end of helping you to grow inwardly by learning to go quietly within, here is a simple but marvelous exercise. I call it the "Thou Art" prayer.

First, find a quiet place to be by yourself. For this particular inner practice, early morning hours are best. Seated comfortably, preferably with your back straight, start by consciously relaxing yourself and then close your eyes.

This prayer begins each time with you silently saying or intoning to yourself the words, "Thou art," and then from there you take the first letter of the alphabet, A, and use it to create the word you'll use to create your prayer. For example: "Thou art the Absolute, Thou art the Almighty," or whatever word comes to you beginning with the letter A that you feel is true of God or His Goodness.

Each time you create and then speak these words, try to feel what that whole idea means to you—the idea of the Absolute, the idea of the Almighty. Then you proceed to the next letter in the alphabet, B. "Thou art the Beginning, Thou art the Breath that I take."

With each passage you mentally and emotionally create, strive to be there with yourself, fully within yourself, and with all that you understand about that Truth you feel. Then move on to the next letter, C. "Thou art the Creator and the created, Thou art the Christ, Thou art Compassion." With each word you choose in this prayer, try to understand or think through everything you know about that ideal. Then proceed ahead, continuing to use the alphabet as the basis for the next Divine attribute you'll bring to mind. "Thou art the Door of Life. (Don't be afraid to add to your prayer anything that feels good and natural to you.) Thou art the Everlasting. Thou art my Friend. Thou art my God. Thou art the Holy of Holys. Thou art the Invincible." Feel completely free to vary this prayer as it naturally occurs to you in the moment of prayer. Go through the alphabet, choosing as many words as you like to match the letter you're sounding out. And what will happen is your mind will become quiet because you're connecting your mind and your

What could be more practical than becoming absolutely fearless?

heart together. You're turning around into yourself by consciously bringing yourself *into* the prayer.

I can't tell you how practical this—or any true prayer— really is. People just don't realize the power that rests within them. Think about it. What could be more practical than becoming an absolutely fearless man or woman? What could be more practical than becoming an individual who understands that you have all the time in the universe, literally. Christ said, "Have I not said ye are gods?" Do you have any idea what understanding this means to you? It has nothing to do with your outer hopes and ambitions, all of which keep you from understanding that who you really are is *within* what you really are . . . and that you must go there to find it.

Prayer is for that purpose. Everything depends on you becoming an inner man and an inner woman. Prayer is what will help you not only to do that, but it will illuminate all those regions within what you are, so that God Himself can come in and take His rightful place in your life—*as* your Life.

Special Lessons for Self-Study

What you receive from this life in each moment is intimately connected to, and ultimately dependent upon, the way you think toward life in that moment.

How else will you learn not to be associated with what you presently are other than through having a conscious relationship with it?

Prayer is a way to enter into and come to know your Self.

People become wrongly frustrated with prayer and meditation when their imagined spiritual pictures of themselves are shaken by the glimpse of their *actual* inner state, at which point they then refuse this rescuing reality.

The reason it is so important to be an inner-oriented man or woman is because inward is where upward begins.

R enew thyself completely each day; do it again, and again, and forever again.

—ANCIENT CHINESE PROVERB

seven

In the life of the Indian there was only one inevitable duty—the duty of prayer—the daily recognition of the Unseen and Eternal. Daily devotions were more important than daily food … Each soul must meet the morning sun, the new sweet Earth, and the Great Silence alone.

—OHIYESA, SANTEE TRIBE

The Secret Power in Practicing Ceaseless Prayer

Once there was a small happy family. Mother and father cared deeply for one another and took special care to see that their young son and daughter developed well-rounded lives. He was somewhat of a self-studying man, and his wife was also interested in the interior life. For this man and woman, life was a continual learning experience. They took nothing at face value. And over the years their children would reflect these values, having had placed within them that Seed of seeds that ensures each would grow up to become a different order of human being, as we'll see.

One of their favorite family activities was exploring the great outdoors, and they all looked forward to when time and circumstance allowed them to take short trips into the back country. This brings our story to one day in the middle of a beautiful May when things worked out so that the whole family could go on a three-day camping trip. Off they went!

The new campsite they had chosen from the rangers trail guide required a simple hike for a mile or two over mostly level terrain. After a one-hour trek following a partially overgrown path, they found themselves all alone in a small clearing where a small beautiful river flowed slowly through a picturesque valley. Fortunately, as it was getting late, a roughed-in campsite awaited them right there at one of the bends in the river. Although the area needed some picking up, all in all it couldn't have been nicer. Filled with fresh air, soothing sounds of running water, lots of unusual rock formations, tall pines in the distance—it was Mother Nature in all of her natural goodness.

Now you know kids, especially when—after having to wait patiently to reach the end of some highly anticipated destination—they finally arrive. They're out of there! There's just too much to see, too much to do. So, while the parents worked to set up camp they heard the children laughing and running around, having a great time exploring their new outdoor home.

About half an hour later the parents heard that the children—who only moments before had been carrying on so happily—had stopped making any sounds at all. A bit concerned, Dad dropped what he was doing and ran down to where the children were both quietly sitting on the pebbled river bank. He saw they looked kind of sad and defeated, so he sat between the two of them, putting his arms around both, and asked his son, "What's wrong, honey?"

"I don't know."

And turning to his daughter: "Well, what's wrong with you, sweetheart?"

"I don't know."

All right, he thought to himself, maybe another tact will take them out of their slump. So he squeezed them both to his side, laughing to get them laughing, "Come on! You guys were having such a good time. What's the story here?"

But silence was all he won for his effort. Another idea hit him. "All right. Tell you what! Let's go up, build a fire, and cook our dinner. Mom's got some great snacks too! Marshmallows and chocolate and graham crackers! How does that sound?"

Sure enough, not too much later—their tummies full from a delicious meal and hands filled with their favorite dessert treats—they forgot their sadness. All seemed well again. But in the back of their father's mind, he was wrestling with the strange unexplained change in his children's behavior by the river.

After the passing of a thankfully uneventful night, the next day brought with it plenty of blue skies, just the right number of shading clouds, and a pleasant seventy-five degrees. Again the kids went down to the bank of the river to play, and just like the day before, their parents heard them laughing and shouting out in those short bursts of over-the-top enthusiasm. Then, all of a sudden, dead silence again. Again the father raced down to where they were playing.

"What's wrong?" he asked. And one more time, in barely audible voices, they both responded, "I don't know."

But this time Dad has an idea. "Well, look. What have you two been up to for the last hour? Because I want to play with you."

Their reply is innocent enough. "We've been making boats."

Visually searching for evidence of their handiwork, and not seeing anything, he asked, "What do you mean, you've been 'making boats'?" Looking around again for clues, only this time taking in the larger picture, he could feel the last piece of the puzzle about to solve itself in his mind. Then it hit him. He saw the whole story. But, just to confirm his growing intuition, he decided to take one last step. Smiling down at them, he said, "I sure would love to see you build your boats. Think you could each make one for me?"

In an instant the kids were laughing again as they ran around gathering up differently shaped sticks, accepting this one and tossing that one as though there was a diagram they were working from. Finally two small ships take shape, each topped off with a little leaf mast for a sail. Then Dad told them, "Okay, time to cast off, you little swabbies! Let's get your boats in the water." With this they both dropped their stick-ships into the water where, in only a moment's time, the river's current began to carry them downstream. Waiting long enough only to see their eventual destination which now confirmed his original suspicion, the father grabbed the hands of his kids and excitedly told them, "Quickly now! Come with me." To which they both immediately protested, "But, Dad . . . what about our boats?!"

"Never mind that for right now," he said. "Just come with me, I want you both to see something special!" And with their hands in his they ran up a small hill at the bend in the river less than a hundred feet down from where the kids had been playing. When they reached its grassy-stubbled top the children could look down

You can't stand on dream planks.

on the whole river, and from *this* vantage point they were able to watch as their small boats drifted slowly down toward them, floated around the bend they now stood atop, and then continued downstream. When their stick-ships had at last become too small to see, they looked up at Dad and smiled at him. And even though neither of them could say why, right at the moment both were grateful for what their father had just shown them.

Do you see what they were able to? What is the lesson in this story? Let's look together.

The first time the children put their little boats in the water, being too young to comprehend their physical surroundings, it appeared to them that their boats had just disappeared. Unable to see down the river past the hill at the bend, they couldn't grasp where their boats had gone. Now, what about you? Have you made the connection yet—how their psychological condition is not unlike your own at certain times?

Have you ever found yourself feeling sullen or sad because you don't know where your little boat has gone? Try to see where this simple story accurately illustrates certain aspects of your day-to-day experiences. Almost every single day there comes a certain sadness because one or more of your boats seems to have disappeared. Maybe these few examples will help bring home the intended lesson.

How about the boat of your dreams? Or that long-awaited docking of your love boat? Are you starting to see the connection here? And just to ensure everyone's aboard, what about that great steamship of what you had planned to do by a certain age? Remember that schedule? By the time I'm thirty, or forty, or fifty, then later by sixty, seventy. That's right, we all keep pushing the age back for our ship to come in. Why? Because those little boats of ours keep going around the bend, disappearing while we watch and wonder what happened.

How about the boat of your dreams?

For reasons we'll continue investigating in this book, we've come to accept as natural a strange and unexamined psychological state of self where just about everything concerning our lives is contained in this next sentence: "*I am not yet, but I will be.*" Let's look at this psychological state closely, "I am not yet, but I will be." What does it mean?

We have some ship at hand, or plans for one, meaning we either succeed at something or some hoped-for achievement is under construction, and so we feel good about ourselves today. Maybe my present sense of well-being is that I just made some money, or my friend agreed that he was wrong and I was right; perhaps at last, she said she'd marry me, or whatever the cause: "I feel good today."

But no more do I get the ship built than it goes around the bend! Translation: *Everything changes!* It seems that I rarely, if ever, get to stand on the bow of my boat and feel the wind at my back for days in a row, enjoying the strength of its sturdy planking, relaxed because my sails are full and I know they'll stay that way. Far from it. *My* ships always seem to disappear. What's really happening? Not all of them run aground and breakup. Where do they go? Please pause long enough here to think through this next important idea and what it means in light of the story about the children's lesson on the hilltop.

Our ships drift and disappear into what we call our *past.* And it needs to be injected here that we don't really have a ship in the future either, except for the one of our dreams. You can't stand on dream planks, can you? No, life's storms see to that! So it seems that much of our own life experience parallels that of the children in our story. Only for us it isn't little stick-ships that disappear. It's one *thought* after another—because in our lives these are the ships.

Thought by thought, we build ourselves these ships and we put them in the water and we go, "Ah." Then it floats away, as it's supposed to, and we watch it proudly for what, in our lifetime, seems but a few minutes. And as long as life events allow us to remain identified with it, we say, "Look at me! I'm a shipbuilder. A good one!" Then that ship goes around the bend, leaving us feeling lost again, without a ship, standing only upon the memory of what once was.

Can you think of certain individuals you know who live almost exclusively in the memory of their ships? What about you? How much time each day is spent walking the decks of ships gone by? That's what we do, isn't it?

"Ah, I remember when they said I could have been champ! When I really was going someplace in this world or, to a lesser extent, how sharp I looked in that new car or when I bought that new coat"—whatever it was. Millions of people live in just this way, walking each day up and down the deck of their ghost ships, reminiscing about what once was or could have been "if only." Most don't even care if these ships have splintered and sunk. How about this one: "I remember when he loved me." All these thoughts and feelings from the past provide you temporary planking to stand on in the present moment.

So, here's the problem: We keep looking for ourselves in these little ships. But why? Because with each and every one of these new ships is born a temporary new sense of self. With each new event we're able to plan or somehow get built, for *that* moment in time, *we feel real.* But where do these events and their equivalent identities come from? Continuing with this metaphor, they seem to come down the river, don't they? You're sitting there, and all of a sudden someone calls you, "Here's a new opportunity!" In that instant you have yourself a grand new boat. Well, that came floating toward you out of the blue, didn't it? Yes, it did. And then a day, week, month, year, or decade later it's gone around the bend, into the impenetrable shadows of that unknown place we call our past.

Thinking about this last idea for a moment, doesn't it seem that everything in our lives comes to us from upriver, meaning that our life events seem to float down toward us on this stream we know as the movement of time? And at a certain point—where you can start to see this possibility in time heading your way—you start *thinking* about it. In an invisible moment later, a new sense of self starts taking shape based on what you think you see, or want to see, and these projections then become *your* ship. Now you feel really worthwhile, because you've got a ship. Then this ship, like the others before it, goes around the bend and now you don't have a "you" anymore. And so it starts all over again, the search for something, any new thing that promises to provide yet another sense of yourself.

Everything changes.

If we can see the truth in this invisible inner drama, then we should also be able to see its inevitable conclusion. We need to realize that whatever that newest thing may be that we're about to invest ourselves in—to derive that longed-for sense of ourselves from—has to be just as empty as all of the other things we've invested ourselves in, otherwise we'll spend the rest of our physical existence just like those children, sending one ship after another down the river, only to feel lost when they go around the bend and disappear.

Admittedly this account would be bad news for all of us *if* it was the end of the story. But if you understand the futility of looking for a permanent sense of yourself in the river of time, it is decidedly *not* the end. It's the start of another story, the potential birth of a whole other world. Here's one way this new world within begins.

Some individuals reach the point in life, a true turning point, where having had so many of their ships disappear, they say at last, "I want to have a relationship with something that *doesn't* disappear on me. I want to find something timeless. I want a *real* relationship with God." If such

We are always trying to build a self that won't disappear.

a thought has already occurred to you, then you also understand why this wish to be connected to that which won't disappear is so important. Grounded within God, *you* won't disappear. Have you thought it through? Men and women want a relationship with the Divine because if they can have a relationship with something that is timeless, then that relationship itself will establish a timelessness within them. That's the whole point.

We are always trying to build a self that won't disappear out of the things that are coming in the stream of time, never understanding that nothing we find floating upon this temporal stream can ever be timeless. And if this is true about the nature of the world's ever-becoming events, how much more impermanent is our sense of identity derived from them? But we're slow to learn! No sooner do we climb aboard that new sought-after sense of self than around the bend it goes. To which we say, "well, OK, that wasn't it!" Have you ever said that before? "No, that wasn't it. But wait! This must be it!" And then you do it all over again?

How can we find that life that doesn't have this perpetual sense of loss in it? Where one day we're the captain of a fine ship, and the next day we can't even find the boat! We don't even have a dinghy! To make matters worse, we aren't even sure what just happened other than we seem to have lost ourselves once again.

The real question in the light of these findings should be: what are the requirements for any of us *to be?* What does it take to keep ourselves from repeatedly going through this experience of loss? And if such a life is possible, how is it to come about for us?

The principal pain of our physical existence, psychologically speaking, is that every single day—and at least ten thousand times in a given life span—there's this dreaded feeling of losing yourself when that little boat that you thought was "you" disappears around the bend. The good news is that as you start to understand the nature of the real problem, you also begin to understand the solution. So, the first part of this necessary knowledge is to see it *is* true, you do lose yourself. And that the way that you lose yourself is through looking for a permanent sense of yourself in a nature that is itself forever disappearing, as its existence arises from and is carried away in the stream of time.

We've covered this before in some ways, but now we're going to touch on it more significantly. Our senses perceive our lives as taking place in a physical world whose nature is just like a river. Life is there outside of us and it just flows by, one event after another. And every event that flows by is filled with things that either supply a solid sense of yourself, or within which you're searching for this sense of self. Every comment someone makes, each car that drives by, even the color of someone's shirt, can provide you with a temporary ship by which to know yourself. This is how we know ourselves and is pretty much our present experience of life: a never-ending series of hopeful beginnings usually followed by some unwanted or dark ending. Why? Once again, that nature within us responsible for our life experience knows only one way to "know" itself—and that is to find itself in what is flowing by.

In short, we're always trying to find a self that is permanent, but the very self that's seeking is impermanent. And within what is perhaps only a dim understanding of our actual spiritual condition we turn and ask in earnest, "How do I find a permanent me?" This brings us to the real purpose of prayer: To connect yourself with and to remain conscious of what is good, timeless, and true whose dwelling place is within you. That permanence is there now. You are its intended, as it should be yours.

Even so, to attain this level of higher consciousness is not without its cost. You have to work to understand, to begin *seeing* that your own thought nature is creating every microsecond a certain false sense of self, and that it's *this self* who always disappears in the stream of time. Once you start to see this Truth, your course of action is implied and immediate. You know that you need a new North Star; something to rely on that doesn't set. You know you need to be connected to something that doesn't disappear when all of the things that you call yourself do. And out of this first little bit of real self-knowledge comes the whole new action of working to remember yourself; of striving inwardly at all times and in all circumstances to be aware of your interior unchanging self even as you move through a world filled with ever-changing events. This brings us to the inner practice of *ceaseless prayer*. A short, personal invocation to God inviting His eternal Being to become as your own.

By far the best prayer of any kind is always the one spoken from the honest, open heart; words that arise from having seen and understood your own true inner condition. There is no better prayer than that. But there are some prayers that can help bring about higher prayers, just as water is sometimes used to dig a well. I'll give you a few examples.

We strive for permanence, but the very self that's seeking is impermanent.

For instance, you might one day realize that part of what's wrong with your life is that there's too much of you in it! That what you really need is more of God, and less of you. Whether this idea resonates with you now (or comes to you later as a necessary step in your spiritual development) and you're unsure as to how to proceed, have no concern how this kind of exchange might take place. It's not your responsibility to fulfill your new wish, only to keep it before you at all times. The following short, simple prayer will prove itself a powerful reminder to help realize your new and higher intention. Whether sitting silently by yourself, in the midst of a hurried day, or moving through throngs of people in the supermarket, quietly continue to consciously repeat these words to yourself: "More of Thee, less of me . . . More of Thee, less of me."

The understanding and the practice of ceaseless prayer is probably timeless itself. Most likely sincere spiritual seekers long, long ago realized that the unattended mind with its thought nature left to its own devices could do nothing but continue creating life in its own temporary image. So, whether lifted by the Spirit to intone their gratitude, or on realizing their total dependence on its ceaseless Being for their own, or from some insight born of their longing for the Almighty to transform their nature, these men and women began the practice of ceaseless prayer. All religions—some more secretly than others—teach this special inner practice as both self purifier and provider.

What's wrong with your life is that there's too much of you in it.

The old desert fathers commonly used the Jesus Prayer which was simply, "Lord Jesus Christ, son of the living God, have mercy on me." In the East one form of this practice is called "Dhikr Allah" or the remembrance of God. They inwardly repeat: "La ilaha ill-Allah," which means, "There is no God, but God."

Another short prayer that is both poignant and makes the point intended in the practice of ceaseless prayer is: "Thou art my God, my only God." Again, this prayer is kept repeating in your mind.

It's excellent inner work for many reasons to connect the movement of your breath with your prayer so that on the in-breath you mentally intone or repeat, "Thou art my God," and on the out-breath, "My only God." Or, as in the first short prayer mentioned, to intone "More of Thee" on the in-breath, and on the out-breath, "less of me."

Working to connect your prayer with your breathing serves many purposes that are a life-long study in themselves. For now, it is enough to point out that just working to be aware of each breath helps ground you in the present moment where Life itself is actually breathing you. The truth is that all things under the sun are tied together in this dynamic expression of living opposites and even the expanding universe is, in scale, the out-breath of the Supreme.

There's one small variation in your prayer practice that may prove itself valuable, particularly if the prayer you choose to work with is too long to comfortably repeat within one side or the other of the natural breath cycle. Whatever your prayer may be, take the first letter from each word of the prayer, for example, "More of Thee, less of me," and work with the phonics of each first letter until you create a word from these letters that's pleasing to your ear. For instance, you've got "More of Thee" as M-O-T—and "less of me," which is L-O-M. So that's M-O-T, L-O-M—More of Thee, less of me. M-O-T, L-O-M.

Now, it just so happens when you sound out M-O-T and allow the letters to blend, they can be shaped to sound like another word: *emote;* an old root word that means "to express." The letters L-O-M are easily sounded out like

"Elohim," one of the words used to mean the angelic radiations or emanations of God in the Old Testament. So in M-O-T, L-O-M, you find a short prayer that not only allows you to work at remembering something that is Timeless, but that in every word and every breath that you take, in each of its short phrases, you can find and relate to newer and deeper meaning within your own deepening self-understanding.

Connect yourself with something outside of time.

All or any one of these short, small prayers and inner-oriented practices can help provide you, as you work at practicing remembering yourself within one of them, with a way in which to connect yourself with Something outside of time, with That which doesn't disappear.

Let me urge you to work at this work of ceaseless prayer. Beginning today, choose to use your life for those true purposes that withstand the test of time instead of allowing your life to be used up serving only one temporary purpose after another. Use every waking moment—when you're eating, while you're walking or just waiting around somewhere for something. Whenever you can remember yourself in whatever you may be doing, bring yourself back into the awareness of the present moment and into that Secret Permanence that dwells therein.

If you're at work you have to do your assigned tasks, but when you take a break, return to that higher awareness that cannot disappear into the river any more than the ocean can be engulfed by one of its own waves. In this state of awareness, the river of time and all on it runs by you and through you instead of carrying you away. In its waves and ripples you can see your own thoughts float by with no sense of loss. This is the essence of spiritual detachment. You choose to stay with what is Timeless by refusing to lose yourself in the world of thought and time. Now, to help strengthen your understanding of the need for this kind of new inner work, I've made the following short list.

Why Work to Pray Unceasingly

An unattended mind is the breeding ground of self-defeat.

Conscious efforts are always rewarded with increased consciousness.

Wasted energies are the same as lost opportunities.

An unattended mind is the breeding ground of self-defeat. What does that mean? If you're not present in your own life, working moment to moment to remember something Timeless, you will find and then lose yourself in every thought or event that floats by. That's what self-defeat is— the unconscious act of being identified with and investing yourself in what must disappear. Then a sense of loss, sorrow or suffering rushes in to fill the temporary gap. Again, an unattended mind is the breeding ground of self-defeat.

Conscious efforts are always rewarded with increased consciousness. Speaking of rewards, where do you think you're going to find the Kingdom of Heaven? It awaits you within increased consciousness, a fact that requires we add something else to this thought. We live within a totally responsive universe, but you need to understand it beyond just the idea of mechanical give and take. The universe always responds with more than you have asked for. And when you begin to ask for real things in life, you get more than you can possibly know you're asking for. So, to increase your consciousness is the same as learning to ask for something more, and to learn to ask for more is to receive more than you could ever imagine. And lastly,

Wasted energies are the same as lost opportunities. And please remember this, it connects with that same level of responsiveness just mentioned above. This life, along with our experience of it, is the living expression of a great universe of opposites from which all forms derive their existence. These opposites never cease to express themselves, even if you don't see their actions. Directly to the point now, when you stop working to grow, you begin dying. Now is it clearer? You should work to pray unceasingly because wasted energies are the same as lost opportunities. If you build and climb aboard a ship of self, and it floats down the river only to disappear, did you not invest your life's energies in something ultimately without lasting value? Did you not have, in the same moment you started to build that ship, the opportunity to place your attention on something that is Timeless? Yes. It's true: Wasted energies are the same as lost opportunities.

Every moment that you can, come wide awake! Do it right now! You'll never know how forgetful of your self you are until you make the smallest effort to be self-remembering. In relationship to your effort to see that self-forgetfulness is overtaking your life, and that it is the real cause of your pain, comes a kind of new and special spiritual memory; a certain Presence that little by little grows in you as a powerful new awareness. As you work to place it before all else in your life, it begins to go before you, not only keeping you from forgetting yourself, but helping you to realize, increasingly, your connection to the Celestial, Timeless Life. So start this wonderful, positive, upward spiral by using ceaseless prayer to go within yourself. You'll quickly discover that this wish to go in is the same as asking to go up! Remember these three powerful reasons why you should work to pray unceasingly.

Become the discoverer of your own secret internal life.

I can't tell you how important it is that you become the investigator, the discoverer of your own secret internal life, and the immense value there is in investing as much time as possible in this spiritual task. How are you ever going to know if there's a Kingdom of Heaven if you spend all of your time investing your energies in the kingdom of earth? How are you going to know if there's something Timeless, if you don't at least try to enter into the world where Timelessness meets it?

Special Lessons for Self-Study

We are always trying to build a self that won't disappear
out of the things that are coming in the stream of
time, never understanding that nothing you can build
in the stream of time is going to be Timeless.

The only pain in this physical existence, psychologically
speaking, is mistaking what is temporary for the
Permanent.

We are always trying to find a self that is permanent, but
the very self that's seeking is itself impermanent.

Choose to stay with what is Timeless by refusing to
lose yourself in the world of thought and time.

An unattended mind is the breeding ground of self-
defeat. Conscious efforts are always rewarded with
increased consciousness. Wasted energies are the
same as lost opportunities.

The most powerful prayer, one well-nigh omnipotent
and the worthiest work of all, is the outcome of a
quiet mind. The quieter it is the more powerful, the
worthier, the deeper, the more telling and more perfect
the prayer is. To the quiet mind all things are possible.
What is a quiet mind? A quiet mind is one which
nothing weighs or worries, which, free from ties and
all self-seeking, is wholly merged into the will of God,
and dead as to its own.

—MEISTER ECKHART

eight

P ray—Period! Don't expect anything. Or
better, expect nothing. Prayer cleanses us
of expectations and allows Holy Will,
Providence, and Life itself an entry. What
could be more worth the effort—or
non-effort!

—THOMAS MOORE

How to Make
All of Life Be Just
for You

How many times have you come
home, maybe from a party or some
business engagement, and upon laying your
head down to rest, became aware of a certain
unwanted feeling? A nagging mental or
emotional state that you recognize
immediately as a familiar visitor? In this
instance, the recognizable visitor we're

151

talking about is that feeling that tends to come around for most of us as regularly as the seasons themselves. Who hasn't felt the chill of doubt-filled thoughts and feelings raining down upon them, asking steadily, "Where am I going? What have I done? What do I really have of my own?" Can you be honest and say "Yes, that's true. I am intimate with these uninvited thoughts and feelings."

To one degree or another, *all* of us are victims of these visitations, the end result of which is the feeling, "Well, what's it all for?" Experiences of this kind come in every shape and size, so don't believe for a moment that the so-called successful are in any way immune. For instance, you can have all the money in the world, and then hear that someone has said something bad about you, and suddenly you're in the grip of thoughts and feelings that are asking and telling you: "What has all that I've got done for me?"

> Failure is when we place our invented intentions over Life's genuine one.

How this sad state of affairs persists in spite of all our efforts to overcome it may be difficult to understand, but it is simple to see. Let me make the point plainly: The way we are presently, it takes virtually nothing to make us feel as though our lives are nothing. One passing shot, the smallest thought of this nothingness erases all the accumulated thoughts of wealth and well-being. Haven't you noticed that? And what's so important for you to grasp in this these opening comments is that you never know when that one thought or feeling—arising out of that one circumstance—is going to come in and strip everything away; when all that you call the work that you've done just disappears, leaving you saying to yourself, "All for nothing."

Now if you're like most well-intentioned men and women, then you do the right thing, but you do it in the wrong way. You decide to start over. That's lesson one. You start over. In a certain sense you won't find a more important prayer than the wish and the willingness to start your life over. But the key here, and where countless souls unconsciously miss the mark, is that you have to start over in the right way. But what do I mean by the "right" way?

How many years are you going to keep telling yourself that it hasn't all been for nothing and that you're learning from your mistakes? Believe me, every single human being on the planet is absolutely convinced, "I am growing from my mistakes!" Please consider the truth in the following insight, even if it goes against what you hope is true: You may be growing in the addition of psychological information that you carry and refer to about yourself, with lots of facts why you'll never run into trouble again. You know the drill, how it always starts with how much you see about the whole business you didn't see before. But the inevitable conclusion to each of these recurring painful life experiences is that you have not learned *the real lesson* behind them, otherwise why their return visit? This also means it's usually just a matter of time until, because of yet some other unforeseen event, you're wondering once again what on earth your life is for.

One of the secret reasons why the spiritual path is so difficult is that it begins in earnest with the new understanding that Life has its own intention, and that real success in life depends on our uncovering this higher intention and aligning ourselves, our actions, with it. So failure, to give it a quick definition, is when men and women place their invented intentions over Life's genuine one. Can we not see that the feeling of "all for nothing again" is the proof that our intention did not align itself with Life's? Otherwise, something different would have occurred. Let me prove that you and I are doing the wrong thing in life with our lives, or at least doing it incompletely. If we can see and understand the fact of the findings that follow, we can start all over and begin working in the right way to receive those real rewards in life that come with being an inwardly awake man or woman.

Everything in life is for something. Everything!

One fact for both our inner education and constant encouragement is that when you know how to look into life, it's possible to find the Celestial in even the most common, natural things. Therein you see that everything in life is *for* something. Let's start there.

Everything in life is *for* something. Everything! The bees. What are the bees for? Well, for one thing, the bees are for flowers, aren't they? They pollinate the flowers. What are the trees for? The trees are for all creatures, to clean the air and provide shade and shelter for the birds, and food for all. And the rain, what's rain for? Well, rain is for the flowers and the trees, the birds and the bees, you and me. I'm only trying to show with these elementary examples that when you look out at life, you can't find anywhere in all of its tremendous web of relationships something within it that isn't for something else. Everything is *for* something.

There's more to this, and it remains simple to see when we'll look with our wish to see. The bees and the flowers, the birds and the trees, the rain and the soil—all of these things that are for one another—complete one another in their "for-ness." Do you understand? Does not the bee complete the flower? Where would the flowers be without the bees? Where would anything be without that thing it completes by being for it? This observable feature of natural life teaches us something vast and vital in our search for God's Life. Allow me to make some of these invisible lessons clear to you.

When you are for the right thing, the thing that you're for and the part of you that's for it *make one complete thing.* Two seemingly disparate elements come together to make a complete "something" that is always more than the sum of its parts. Call it a circle in nature. One thing is *for* something else that it needs, and the thing that it's for is *for* it because it needs it; when the two are together, when the "for" meets the "need," you have something that is made whole or complete. Do you understand? The tree branch needs leaves and is for them, just as the leaves need the branch and are for it. Both branches and leaves are for the tree that supports them, just as the tree is for them. Apart from one another, they have no existence. For one another, life thrives. It sounds simple. It is, yet it's not. What we are witnessing when we look at the birds and the bees and the flowers and the trees, all that business . . . what we're looking at in a physical sense, in this visible world, is just a tiny portion of the greater invisible Real World.

You can't begin to change the kind of human being you are until you start to understand that you live in a world that is, by and large, ten thousand times greater in its invisibility than its visibility. This great dynamic of things that are for one another, and that complete one another in an unseen web of life, speaks of an invisible relationship at work going on around us all of the time. And the first key point to be made here is that when we're for the right thing in this life we get the right reward, which is the joy of feeling ourselves more complete. Another way of restating this same happy result, and perhaps better said, is that we finally lose that terrible sense we have of feeling ourselves as being apart and incomplete.

In that split second when you do something right for another human being, when you know you shouldn't hurt someone with your angry tones or cruel remarks and abstain from yourself at the cost of yourself, when you know you shouldn't spend money that you don't have or even that you do have, when you do the right thing for yourself, you receive the reward of doing the right thing. The reason you get that reward is because you were *for* the right thing. Your conscious action completes you in that split second. And in that exact same split second, you also receive the encouragement to do the right thing again, which is another kind of reward in itself!

Let's return for just a moment to that particular problem we identified at the beginning of this chapter. Remember it? It was that recurring experience of feeling as though "all has been for nothing." Let's see how learning to be *for* the right thing in life is the same thing as freeing ourselves from this unwanted inner visitor.

One of the ways we incorrectly deal with these moments of wondering "what's it all for?" is that we push away our own feelings of futility by telling ourselves, "Well, this is just something I have to go through." Please don't misunderstand me. You see, the fact of the matter is, it *is* something you have to go through. But the other unseen fact of life is that you're not supposed to go through the same thing 50,000 times! It is *not necessary* to go through painful self-doubt 50,000 times! You're not supposed to hate someone 50,000 times and then—feeling the separation and sense of self-isolation that the hatred causes you—follow it up by telling yourself, "I know better than to do that because Christ (or Mohammed, Buddha, or the Great Mother, or whomever) said I should be different." And then, because you've identified yourself with something outside of yourself that you hope is greater than your weakness, or you've pounced on yourself (to punish yourself to prove to yourself you're sorry) you believe in this moment that next time you're going to be different. But you're not! And as rightfully humiliating as this lesson may be, it's

Learn to be for the
right things in life.

important for us to come to terms with the time-proven truth of it. Here is one more example before we move on.

If I asked you how many of the same "loops" have you gone through in your life, you'd know more or less what was being implied, wouldn't you? Sometimes these unwanted life-loops take less than a minute, swearing to yourself, "never again," even as you begin that self-compromising cycle yet once more. Sometimes these losing loops can take a month or even years. What about the career loop? Or certainly one of the most painful loops of all, the relationship loop? Where, much to your disbelief, you find yourself right back where you started. You know the story! He's completely dependable, much different than the one before; or she seemed so caring, she'd never betray your trust. Then you hear yourself crying out, "Oh no!" And because you don't realize the real reason why you're back "there" again ("there" being that same feeling you didn't want to feel last time), you make the same mistake you made the time before: You are *still* for the wrong things in life. Deeply consider the truths revealed in these last paragraphs in the light of the next sentence. See if its timeless promise doesn't ring with new assurance.

> **B**efore the Truth can set you free, you must be for the Truth.

Before the Truth can set you free, *you must be for the Truth.* But we don't really understand what this Truth means as it concerns our everyday lives and their various affairs. We lack this essential spiritual knowledge because every time we encounter a moment when there's no denying we've been for the wrong thing, up pops a certain all-knowing part of us and pronounces, "Ah yes . . . it's clear. I see it all now! I know what went wrong this time." And we buy it! The self that's talking to us has our complete confidence. We've no doubt it knows what to be for and how it's going to change everything next time around. Balderdash!

Something must happen to us where we realize our actual condition, where one fateful day we say to ourselves something like, "Look at this! For five, ten, twenty, even forty years, I've struggled to escape this circle of myself, to become a different kind of human being, and I'm still going through these loops. I'm no more able to bring myself a new life than the fall can bring itself closer to spring!" And I tell you when you no longer push away the fact of *that*, when you know you've run out of all explanations—all "whys" for the way you are—you're ready for the first time to do something that you have never done before. You are ready to be for something which, by you being for it, *will change you.*

Once upon a time there was a distant world known throughout the cosmos for its unique race of beings who lived and worked there, generally playing out their lives doing the best they knew how. Perhaps the most unique feature of the people inhabiting this planet was that beginning around the age of three or four, all these beings naturally grew a special organic apparatus on either the right or left side of their forehead. It resembled a kind of headset with a small mirror configured to extend just far enough to allow each person to be able to see him or herself within it.

Try to picture it. This mirror, with its polished surface turned in toward each person's face, set at the proper distance and angle of reflection, allowed each and every citizen to always be looking at their favorite person! But this was just one of its fascinating features. You could also look in this mirror and, with no real effort on your part, see someone who will always be there to give you direction, show you your choices, even evaluate you. Are you starting to grasp the mental picture being drawn out here?

This "off-world" story is a metaphor for the way a certain part of our present nature never stops looking at or thinking about *itself.* Talk about an endless relationship! Bring yourself into our story. It's true, isn't it? You're never alone even if you're the only one in your bed. Thoughts of one kind or another are always present, guiding you, appraising you, pressing to fill in every space every split second. Aargh! Right? Well, that's exactly the life the poor beings in our story had with their built-in self-reflectors. However, as it is for some of us on our planet, on that world the hero of our story, whom we're about to meet, just couldn't help seeing himself differently. Even though almost everyone he knew seemed satisfied enough with their lives, try as he might, he could not stop thinking to himself, "Something isn't right!"

For many years he had been going through certain experiences, just like you and I have had, of day in and day out being for this and being for that; and each new thing that he was for was the promise of his next fulfillment. But nothing that he was for would bring him that contentment his heart yearned for. One day he said, "My God, where does it end? I can't find what I'm looking for in this mirror of mine, but the only place I know to look is in the mirror." He felt betrayed. So this man in our story joined groups like M.A. (Mirrors Anonymous). It was for people who were tired of looking in the mirror! He tried everything, but nothing changed.

Then one day he saw an innocent looking ad in the local paper. It simply said, "Tired of looking in the wrong place?" And without knowing exactly why it moved him, the simplicity of these words appealed to him. He made up his mind to go to one of the advertised meetings.

Tired of looking in the wrong place?

When he arrived there were only a few others in attendance, which made him feel all the more unsure of himself. Besides juggling his own growing doubts, he wasn't at all sure that he liked what he felt was the too-serious tone of the speaker. But he wanted help more than he wanted to hear only what he wanted to hear, so he paid close attention to all that was being said. This is what he heard:

"*You must learn to be for something other than what you are presently for.* But before you can hope to undertake this necessary and life-changing action for yourself, you must understand that the way you presently are, there is a part of you that can't be for anything else until you put something *before* it. This alone is what will work for you, if you will work at it." The speaker paused, looked around the small group for a moment, reading the various faces, and then he continued. "Here's how to begin. Please listen closely.

"All of us are created with a specialized feature. It is within and through this," he continued as he pointed up to the mirroring system on his own head, "that we're able to see ourselves. I want you to place on this mirror of yours one small thought of your own, some simple phrase or little prayer like, 'Thou are the One' or 'My life belongs to You,' or 'More of Thee, less of me.' The point is to place something up in that mirror, so that each and every time you look into it, you will still see yourself, but each time you look there you'll also see what you've deliberately placed there to help remind you that you're supposed to be looking somewhere else.

"And," the speaker added to his talk, "Even if you see the wisdom in this new spiritual prescription and decide to try this new exercise, let me tell you something else you need to know." Again he paused, clearly waiting for the right words to come to him. It seemed a long moment before he spoke again.

"There are unknown parts of you that will do all sorts of things so that you not only forget this exercise, but even why you were working at it in the first place. Because that's the nature of this self-reflecting, mirror-loving nature of ours. But," he continued with carefully measured sentences, "perhaps after a day or two of having forgotten your new intention to look someplace else besides to yourself—when you get tired of feeling the emptiness of having only

Our minds do not belong to us. They belong to themselves.

yourself to look at—you'll remember; and when you do, then just start over. Put something back up in the mirror to help you remember your new Aim. And do this over, and over, and over again; work with your new intention until something begins to happen within you that can't be said with words, but which you yourself will gratefully come to understand."

With this last thought, the speaker took a deep breath and looked directly into the eyes of our unhappy would-be hero. In that instant a contact was made. And then, as if speaking directly to him, the gentleman leading the meeting closed the session with these words:

"When you begin to be for God, for Truth, *before* you're for yourself, God, Truth, will begin to be there before *you.* This Supreme Nature will start to live inside of you and do something that you've never been able to do for yourself. Which is what? Give you the feeling that—at long last— everything is right within you because now the whole of you is *for* the right thing."

Let me shed some additional light on this new form of inner exercise and special prayer. Our minds are, for all intents and purposes, completely undisciplined. What I mean by this isn't that we can't concentrate when needful, or that we are untrained in one skilled mental activity or another. Undisciplined refers to the fact that our minds do not belong to us. *They belong to themselves.* Our task is simply to see the truth of this strange psychic self-centeredness, and then to consciously put something else in the "mirror" so that when the mind goes through what it goes through, and our attention turns to look upon the screen of our thoughts, in that instant we will also see upon—or within it—some small prayer that helps awaken us to what it is that *we really want* to be for in that moment. Perhaps an illustration will help make things clearer.

A spy living in a hostile country once devised a secret way to communicate with his own headquarters. Anyone who knew the special deciphering code could easily read his hidden communication. Here's how it worked. The one receiving his report read the secret contents by pulling out of the message all its first and seventh letters. Running these letters together formed words, and in this way his report got through. For years this agent's unique *message within a message* alerted the allies of the enemy's plans. His efforts were later credited with helping to win the war.

Consciously placing a short prayer within your own thoughts, and working to keep it there, helps to keep you from seeing only the content of your usual thoughts. This short, repeated supplication works like a message within a message, only when you see it there, within your own thoughts, its presence reawakens you to remember that you want to remember something Higher.

We discussed a few of these small personal prayers in an earlier chapter, and again, the best prayer for you is the one with the most personal meaning. However, to refresh your memory, recall these suggested short phrases: "Be Thou my life"; "More of Thee, less of me"; "Thou art my only." The purposeful placing of these or any heartfelt prayers upon the mirror of your mind—along with your intention to let their direction become your own—will turn your whole life around by helping you to be *for* what is genuinely *for* you.

Let me make one last point. What is eating for? What are relationships for? And what about a career or money? Even holding the hand of someone you love? Are you sure? Won't you consider that there may be another purpose; something beyond our present conditioned beliefs that just mechanically accepts what these—and all other—aspects of our lives are for? And when—*if*—you'll consider this question, please add to it this one other important bit of understanding: you and I have already been *for* 10,000 things in this life, and none of the 10,000 things we've been for have really done one thing *for* us, except to give us the vain hope that maybe the next day being for something different will at last change us.

Are you for the Truth?

Begin today, this moment, to use your whole life—every moment of it—to be for something that is in reality *for* you. So that when you're eating, when you're walking, when you're talking, when you're doing whatever you're doing, you have your small unceasing prayer before you. Even if life starts to run away with you, keep your prayer running through you. Keep it right there on the mirror of your mind so that in the middle of any conversation or event you can look up and let it remind you of your wish to be for something Higher.

Truth teachings have long told us that our task is to be for Something Else. And to begin using your life being for Something Else means in this instance, to understand the mechanical operation of the mind, the mirror, the thought process—and to place something in it so that when you go to it and look for yourself in it, you don't just see it. Instead you'll see what has been deliberately placed there by you to remind you to look Someplace Else. This exercise and the new awareness it generates will help you to remember to be for God. It will also help you start seeing that what you are presently for is not what you believe it to be. In this sense it is very accurate to say that what you love does not love you. But everything can be different, and this difference begins with being honest.

What you are presently for is not what you believe it to be.

You can say to someone, "Are you for the Truth? Are you for God?" And usually, in one way or another, that person will indicate, "Yes, I am."

And then you might say, "But honestly, what about today? Were you for the Truth, for God, while you were eating?"

"No."

"Were you for the Truth, for God, when you were driving your car or cutting the lawn?"

"No."

"Were you for the Truth, for God, during those natural breaks in your usual business either at your office or in the home?"

"No."

"Well then, how about when you went for your morning walk or while you were waiting for the bus? Were you for the Truth, for God, during these times?

"Not really."

"Well, when were you for the Almighty One?"

"Oh, after I was weak again I was for Him. Upon hearing the bad news, He was in my thoughts. When I went home and looked at my day and saw that I had been for ten thousand things and that none of them was for me, I called for His help."

The point is more than made. We must each work to be for the Life of Truth—for God's Life—at all times. And this new wish, along with our willingness for it to be our will, must be before us twenty-four hours a day so that it can remind us twenty-four hours a day of what everything is for.

There's one last thing that must be told: The most wonderful fun in the world—true spiritual fun—is to begin developing this new and higher relationship with Life. When you start to understand that what lies ahead of you, in what you've always thought of as your future, isn't really *ahead* of you at all, but waits *within* you—you will be *for* That.

Working with this, and all of the special spiritual exercises you've read in this book, will show you both the need for self-change as well as how to invoke it. The first change in you will be a growing sense of healthy spiritual humiliation, because you'll begin seeing that you can't remember to be for anything but what you have always mistaken as yourself! Oh, what a wonderful discovery it is to see that your present mind is only for itself, and that its nature is actually against what your heart longs for, which is to be whole; to be a new and complete spiritually awake human being.

Special Lessons for Self-Study

You can't begin to change the kind of human being you are until you start to understand that you live in a world that is, by and large, unimaginably greater in its invisibility than its visibility.

Failure is when men and women place their invented intentions over Life's genuine one.

The feeling that everything is right with your life comes in direct proportion to you being for everything that is right in life.

When you're for the right thing, the thing that you're for—and the part of you that's for it—make one complete thing.

Before the Truth can set you free from yourself, you must be for the Truth more than you are for what you've always mistaken as being your self.

The individual soul should seek for an intimate union with the soul of the universe.

— NOVALIS

nine

If we could penetrate to the eternal reality of our own being we would find the one and only solution for every situation in the right sense of our own existence, primarily in itself.

—MAURICE NICOLL

High Lights to Help Brighten Your Journey Home

In this life, in due time, in one form or another, and more or less as you've conceived it, you will receive what you ask for. Of this there's no question. Therefore, learn to guard what you request because nothing conceived, or otherwise created, can satisfy the soul save the Creator who cast your soul from Himself.

171

Denying the day-to-day evidence of your existence doesn't change its fact: emptiness speaks louder than insistence. So based upon your discoveries, re-establish your priorities.

Dare to put aside all relationships other than those serving to reveal what is essential to your real desire. Then, and only then, will what you want from this world be the same as wanting that Essential Relationship for which you have been created and to which you are called. When all you know and see and hope to ask for is God; when He is all you want, you will never know the need to ask for anything ever again.

Study the following 120 special insights and higher inner-life principles closely. Nothing is more valuable than the personal inner work you do to realize that one great relationship called God. Thomas Traherne, English poet and theologian, agrees and encourages you as well: "The contemplation of Eternity, maketh the Soul immortal."

**Every expectation
is a form of prayer.**

It isn't that you need to expand
the world you live in;
you need to be released
from the one you're in!

You find truth by living for its sake.

God, Truth, Reality wants you to wake up from
the whole notion that there's anyone there by
your name that can be made a victim by
anything because His relationship with you,
and yours with Him, lifts you above that.

The barrier that you feel in your prayer
life is a real barrier to the level of self that
experiences it. But there is a reality that
transcends or that is greater than that
self and that level.

Finding the True Powers needed to
take control of your life begins
with understanding the false
powers now in charge of your life.

**Everything you want
to change into
secretly perpetuates
what you want to
change from.**

It is thought's principal preoccupation
to have something always just exceeding
its grasp or in its hands that doesn't
fulfill it so that even as it reaches
—or holds—it must again
have something "new"
to reach for.

To understand how to get out of the
circle of self, you must see completely
into the circle of self; because once you've seen
completely into it, you understand
the system has nothing inside of it that
is for who you really are and what
you really want.

A nature that tends toward taking the easy way,
and the authority that this
tendency creates, has produced our
psychological condition where we
believe ourselves to know,
but really don't.

**We've become complacent creatures
instead of awake human beings.**

**The self that responds
to the challenge or the crisis
is itself a creation of the crisis.**

The nature of the stressed self that
responds to the crisis is itself a creation of the
crisis, which means its vested
interest is in the continuation
of the crisis experience.

When you begin to actively explore
the mystery of your own mystery,
God himself solves the case.

Since it is possible to see your past
pains as having been unnecessary, this means
that the depth of your present
unhappiness is in proportion to your willingness
to be self-deceived.

The fear of seeing the depth
    of your own self-deception
    is the first self-deception.

The nature of thought is that it can only know
itself by peering into itself—an
action that causes separation
even as it seeks to unify.

Freedom is never a condition borne
out of any state of affairs,
but is the fruit of
real relationship.

Each of us potentially lives in at least three
worlds—outer, inner, and those worlds that are
unknown to us because of the deteriorated
condition of the inner world. We don't really
belong to the outer world as evidenced by our
treatment of it, and we don't belong to the
inner world as evidenced by our ignorance of it.
So in effect we are cut off from life, separated
from the worlds we live in, and increasingly by
the very nature of our situation.

**It is only the Light when
it lights your way.**

Better a drop of truth
than an ocean of lies.

An impulse to do good comes from good and,
once rejected, becomes an undetected
susceptibility to evil.

No intention, regardless of how high,
how noble, can be any stronger for you
than your ability to remember it.

On the spiritual mountain, only the
unmarked path leads to the top.
It is the untried way
that is the true one.

The spiritual lesson
that's hardest learned
is that what you have borrowed
must be returned.

The compulsion to teach someone else
his or her lesson in life
is the same as having
refused your own.

The real lessons in life are always delivered
in the moment of honest self-seeing and
this seeing includes the discovery that
something within yourself is trying to
steal these lessons from you.
Refusing any life lesson is the same as
refusing the responsibility for those parts
of yourself that are the problem.

Dependency is any compulsive reliance
upon something not native to your essence
that provides you with a temporary
familiar sense of yourself.

The only possible complete independence in
this world is in being utterly dependent upon
God, for this relationship alone is freedom from
all attachments, including the father of them
all—thought.

For many years in your spiritual life you will
have to decide whether to seek Truth or security,
for in the early stages of the soul's development,
these two things are mutually exclusive. In the
soul's fulfillment these two
become as one.

No addiction of any kind begins
without temptation, but the secret essence
of temptation is to try and complete yourself,
which means that you are resisting your own
sense of being incomplete. Therefore,
temptations are the promises that arise
from the will of that which is
incomplete within you.

How I think I should feel can only
occur to me from the content
of my past experience—and the
content of my past is what's secretly
behind my present sense of feeling
myself incomplete.

The surrender borne of unresolvable crisis in a man is when all possibilities suggested by all parts of him to complete himself are seen as untenable. So he is "delivered from" himself; from the unconscious tyranny of his own parts he is brought into a new awareness of self whose key feature is an inner peace and confidence that has no opposites. He is unified.

Part of self-awakening leads the individual to the point where he is left with the experience of himself that, having been stripped of its longing for experience through either attraction to pleasure or resistance to pain, is then known directly with no intermediating reasons for its nature. Here the experiencer is its own experience, and the only way beyond this is to die to itself, which it does, seeing its own empty content.

Nothing in time can rescue you
from the time nature offering you
that way out.

**You cannot escape yourself;
   you must be rescued from it.**

You must learn to give yourself nothing
but your understanding
of your actual condition.

**We are fulfilled by our need
   to fulfill the need of God.**

The principal reason you can never really
teach anyone else about the true spiritually
based life is because this new life appears only as
each person outgrows being fascinated with his
own present life experiences.

You must be willing to die for what you love
to find out that the only death there is . . . is to
have no love worth dying for.

**When you are willing to die for what you
love, all that dies within you is
what isn't love.**

Most people are so in love with their own
feelings of being loving, they never notice that
they love nothing save themselves and that this
"self" that loves and is so loved is nothing
but illusion.

Every person rightly believes in greater
possibility, but the wise one pursues
it now.

You can't be taken over by an inner
dialogue that you don't have.

There is a Will that includes a balance of
the opposites, and then there is
human's will that exists because of
the opposites.

To accept any spiritual truth as Light
without carrying it into the darkness of yourself
to verify it for yourself is to live
in uncertainty that is fear.

No one can be more than what God wants him or her to be.

What very few see is that life lives itself—and you must be more than life if you want to live. True spiritual principles fail you because you're using them for the wrong purpose at the wrong time. True principles are not for your protection, but to place you where you can see that there is no such self that is in danger. True principles are not intended to keep you safe in battle. They are intended to help you enter into it.

New life lessons appear only in the ashes of old ones.

What we fear invariably is the loss of self
as we know it. When we understand that
to protect this sense of self is the same as
protecting fear—we know that the self
that wants to protect itself is a secret partner
in this fear. *Then* we know
what we must do.

Increase a person's pocketbook, or otherwise
enhance his image of himself, and you produce
a temporary positive result that has inherently
within it its own inevitable opposite, due to,
if nothing else, just the way the world changes
as it's washed clean by the back and forth tides
of time. But, increase this person's spiritual
understanding, and you give to him that which
time is not only powerless to diminish, but that
in fact empowers him over the adverse changes
inherent in time.

Blame does not work. *Any* solution based in blame only postpones the inevitable moment when you will have to blame again. There is nothing to blame for why you feel as you do outside of what you have yet to understand about yourself.

Anger cannot thrive without an object or person to blame for its presence, but if you begin to understand that your anger toward others can't take place without *you* first having misperceived either that person's nature—or the nature of your relationship with them—then you would stop looking in the direction your anger says is its cause and start seeing that the problem really lies in the shallowness of your present self-understanding. This reversal of where you place your attention is the seed of a new struggle whose gradually ripening fruit is freedom from all negative states.

What is the Truth can never be spoken nor
can it be written down.
For you to understand it,
it must possess you.

**Having anything to fall back upon
in this life is to have already
taken the fall.**

Usually understood, exercises are a means to an
end. But real spiritual exercises are a means to a
means—a way to create special conditions in
and under which it is possible to see something
unexpected; to learn the unknown about
ourselves. This special self-seeing can be thought
of as the purpose of the Work, but even it is the
means to the awakening of Intelligence
which serves itself to its own end.

In one of those paradoxes of the spiritual path,
the more aware you are—the more you seem
to fail in life—even as you are less and less
distraught over your weaknesses.

**Moment by moment, every human being
on earth is creating what every other
human being is inheriting.**

We suffer over not fulfilling our mechanical,
unconscious, socially mandated sense of
responsibility, and, so driven, fail to fulfill
our true responsibility, which is to wake up
from our mechanical, unconscious,
socially structured nature.

**Fear of any inadequacy is
the inadequacy feared.**

It is often the conditions we find ourselves in
that determine the inner work we can do, but it
is equally true that it is the work we will do that
changes our conditions.

An invisible string of empty purposes hangs
around the neck of every human being,
but it is never realized as such because
each emptied purpose is replaced with the
promise of yet the next one.

The nature of the obstacles you meet in life
are what they are because of the prize that
you pursue. The self cannot overcome
self-created obstacles, but only re-creates them
with every seeming victory.

When you really begin to pray in earnest to
awaken to His Life, God does not reward you
with the increased strength you're looking for,
but rather with increased insight into your own
weaknesses that eventually become the seed of
the strength you seek as your discoveries cause
you to disappear to yourself.

The greatest lie on earth: "I ache therefore I am real."

You have to understand the prison of self before you can hope to escape it, otherwise everything you do to get out from behind its bars only strengthens the illusion of your captivity.

There is nothing you can do to make God act toward you because He is without cause, yet *knowing this* you must act as if you don't, for although He may be without cause, He is not without compassion.

Awareness is the only cup that can draw from the present moment, while thought draws its life from pools of the past.

To be spiritually asleep is to be
unconscious of your relationship
with life in the moment.

The mind must use its own reasoning to reach
the understanding that it can neither create nor
reach heaven through reasoning.

Refuse to weigh yourself by this world—
rather weigh in against the whole
notion that who you are is
measurable by anyone,
including yourself.

Fear is the blood in the body of mediocrity.

Any step taken in fear toward a fear
reduces that fear by the length of the step
so taken. And any fear reduced in this fashion
never gains what it has lost.

It's not what anyone possesses in life
but rather what he loves
that determines his wealth.

The life of Christ shows that you can't know
perfect freedom without will,
yet it is the surrender of will
that grants freedom.

Something lives within me that is aware
of me—Something that is not me
yet is more me than I am to myself.

Concerning poverty: only from nothing
can God make something
out of you.

Life is not asking you questions—it is giving you the answers!

We turn our pains into questions in order to avoid seeing the answer that they are.

Freedom from what is unwanted by us begins by awakening to what is unknown within us.

There is no other moment but *now* for your inner work. Not working now—not being awake to and in the present moment—is the same as never coming to know why it's always too late to change.

The upward path is inward, which means that it begins and ends within what you *already* are.

We have to imagine what life is for with
all of its various events because we
don't know what we are for.

You may choose your life experience, or not,
but either way, what you are—and what you are
becoming—will not be wasted by the universe.

Spiritually speaking, we are all David trying
in our confusion to become Goliath.

The reason Truth is a pathless land is
because the spiritual journey is not
taken in steps.

Honesty takes wholeness.

If you'll just remember that Real Intelligence
cannot get anxious, then when you're anxiously
looking around for an intelligent action,
you'll know the wise thing to do is
to drop that stupidity.

Eagles do not fear sharks because ocean
predators are not a part of their skyward world.

Stay with what you know is true about any dark
condition instead of letting that dark condition
tell you what is true about you.

It is always possible to see the darkness of any
negative state, which proves that there is
something amidst the darkness that
is not a part of it.

Your true spiritual responsibility is not how you arrive but that you continually set out upon the journey.

The only condition that you ever face is your own level of understanding.

Purpose must define action, otherwise every act is random. When randomness rules, then entropy tries to resolve entropy, resulting in unseen deeper and deeper chaos.

The only thing in life that will never give out beneath you is having nothing to stand on.

The person who thinks that it is
a mistake to speak about truthful concerns
because greater minds than his have already
done so, or tried and failed, does himself an
immeasurable disservice. Just as there is but one
great ocean with innumerable rivers and streams
running into it, so there is but one Great Mind,
and any who learn to ask may mingle with it,
earning access to yet uncharted regions where
deep and sweet waters yet untasted wait to
be poured out.

Only human beings can get pumped up about how humble they are.

Nothing in life doesn't disappear into something
greater than the nothingness into which it slips.

Life is an outpouring: a holy trinity of from,
into, and out again operating on a scale
beyond the time senses.

There are some mysteries beyond even the
greatest thought's ability to grasp. For instance,
how the tree longs for water, detests the
drought, but can't imagine the liberation
in the flame that consumes it. We don't want
the spiritually dry periods and try to hold onto
the vestiges of saturated memories. However,
before the soul can be inflamed, it must be
dried by the stark light of Truth.

The nature of what God notices about you is
completely different than the nature of what
you do to get noticed.

Deliberate acts of rebellion against what you hold dear endears you to God.

We abjectly refuse the notion that many of our unwanted experiences of life are actually our experience of life's justice.

One of the twin bitter fruits of any closed system of thought is unseen arrogance and the self-righteousness that it seeds.

The difference between striving to be right
and refusing to go along with what is wrong is
subtle, but spiritually significant. Striving to
be right in life is an act of will requiring much
thought and struggle. Refusing to go along with
what is wrong is a question of awareness and is
based in surrender. The former path crystallizes
the self by creating the alternating sensations of
victory and defeat, while the latter path releases
the self into its native and eternal Intelligence.

Any event can shatter a belief but, because
of the nature of thought, the shattered belief
itself just becomes yet another belief. Only
insight can shatter a believer by revealing that
neither does such a self exist in reality nor
does reality require one.

All ideas are metaphors, themselves shadows of reality and regardless of subtlety still forms of matter so that beliefs, which are ideas structured to convey meaning from the past, must then be shadows cast from shadows; powerless forms of matter and incapable of delivering anyone to Formless.

Perfect clarity is perfect sanity.

The true and final flowering of insight is humiliation—and its fruit is love.

Insight always reveals evidence of a new and higher order that, by its advent, replaces the former one.

Self-pity is the campsite of self-defeat; it
is a dark refuge for those parts of us
that would rather dwell in what
cannot be than dare to explore
what is possible.

Only the path of self-reliance can bring a person
to full reliance on God.

If you've never felt quietly ashamed of yourself
in a moment of knowing that you've just made
the world a worse place, then you've not yet
begun your spiritual work.

Before you can learn to fear no evil, you
must have no evil fearing.

The perfect equality in God's Kingdom is that
each who enters receives his share according to
his capacity to share; in this fashion each
receives all there is.

Just as there are tides in the seas—invisible
forces which set themselves into the waters
and cause their ebb and rise—so too are there
tides in the silence, forces at work moving
through the quieted mind which give rise
to thought without being touched by it.

The true spiritual, deeply religious life is all
about willingly losing ourselves; being released
into Something beyond anything measurable
by deliberately bringing ourselves to that
interior shore where who we are disappears
because of what we see.

All things good come to those
  for whom the Good is all things.

Religion is the first thing and the last thing, and until a man has found God and been found by God, he begins at no beginning, he works to no end.

—H. G. WELLS

Whenever I Turn from Thee

Please Father
Whenever I turn from Thee, Remind me
Of what I already know
. . . About empty places
And vacant faces . . .
The cost of rushing and finally reaching
Nowhere to go.

Please Father
Whenever I turn from Thee, Remind me
What this world holds without You
. . . Smoldering desires
And laughing liars . . .
The deep despairing of souls still clinging
To life untrue.

Please Father
Whenever I turn from Thee, Remind me
I have nothing of my own
. . . But uncertain footsteps
To constant regrets . . .
That all worth finding rests fully abiding
In You alone.

—GUY FINLEY

A Special Note to the Reader

To receive your free inspiring poster, *10 Ways the Love of Truth Gives You a Fearless Life*, as well as free information about Guy Finley's books, tapes, and ongoing classes, send a self-addressed stamped envelope to:

Life of Learning Foundation
P.O. Box 10P
Merlin, Oregon 97532

Plus, you can receive a free copy of Guy Finley's powerful pocket guide book, *30 Keys to Change Your Destiny*. This amazing 28-page pocketbook of self-development exercises is filled with fascinating self-discoveries and help that work immediately. Send a self-addressed stamped envelope to the address above and please include $1 for shipping and handling. Outside the U.S., please send $3 U.S. funds.

Help spread the Light. If you know of someone who is interested in these Higher Ideas, please send his or her name and address to the Life of Learning Foundation. The latest list of Guy Finley's books, booklets, audio and video tapes will be sent to them. Thank you!

LOOK FOR THE CRESCENT MOON

Llewellyn publishes hundreds of books on your favorite subjects! To get these exciting books, including the ones on the following pages, check your local bookstore or order them directly from Llewellyn.

ORDER BY PHONE

- Call toll-free within the U.S. and Canada, 1-800-THE MOON
- In Minnesota, call (612) 291-1970
- We accept VISA, MasterCard, and American Express

ORDER BY MAIL

- Send the full price of your order (MN residents add 7% sales tax) in U.S. funds, plus postage & handling to:

  Llewellyn Worldwide
  P.O. Box 64383, Dept. K276-3
  St. Paul, MN 55164–0383, U.S.A.

POSTAGE & HANDLING

(For the U.S., Canada, and Mexico)

- $4.00 for orders $15.00 and under
- $5.00 for orders over $15.00
- No charge for orders over $100.00

We ship UPS in the continental United States. We ship standard mail to P.O. boxes. Orders shipped to Alaska, Hawaii, The Virgin Islands, and Puerto Rico are sent first-class mail. Orders shipped to Canada and Mexico are sent surface mail.

International orders: Airmail—add freight equal to price of each book to the total price of order, plus $5.00 for each non-book item (audio tapes, etc.).

Surface mail—Add $1.00 per item.

Allow 4–6 weeks for delivery on all orders.
Postage and handling rates subject to change.

DISCOUNTS

We offer a 20% discount to group leaders or agents. You must order a minimum of 5 copies of the same book to get our special quantity price.

FREE CATALOG

Get a free copy of our color catalog, *New Worlds of Mind and Spirit*. Subscribe for just $10.00 in the United States and Canada ($30.00 overseas, airmail). Many bookstores carry *New Worlds*—ask for it!

Visit our web site at www.llewellyn.com for more information.

The Intimate Enemy
Winning the War Within Yourself

GUY FINLEY
AND ELLEN DICKSTEIN, PH.D.

Within each of us lurk invisible psychological characters that inhabit our inner beings and make choices for us—choices that repeatedly cause us pain on some level. Now, best-selling self-help author Guy Finley and psychologist Dr. Ellen Dickstein expose these characters for what they really are: our mechanical, unconscious reactions and misperceptions that create a threatening world.

The Intimate Enemy will introduce you to astounding parts of yourself that you never knew existed. You will observe the inner dramas that control your life without your knowledge. Best of all, you will awaken to a higher awareness that provides the only true strength and confidence you need to walk into a fearless future. As you uncover the exciting truth about who you really are, you will gain an unshakable understanding of the human struggle and witness proof of a higher world, free from all strife.

1-56718-279-8
5³⁄₁₆ x 8, 256 pp., softcover $9.95

Designing Your Own Destiny
The Power to Shape Your Future
GUY FINLEY

This book is for those who are ready for a book on self-transformation with principles that actually work. *Designing Your Own Destiny* is a practical, powerful guide that tells you, in plain language, exactly what you need to do to fundamentally change yourself and your life for the better, permanently.

Eleven powerful inner life exercises will show you how to master the strong and subtle forces that actually determine your life choices and your destiny. You'll discover why so many of your daily choices up to this point have been made by default, and how embracing the truth about yourself will banish your self-defeating behaviors forever. Everything you need for spiritual success is revealed in this book. Guy Finley reveals and removes many would-be roadblocks to your inner transformation, telling you how to dismiss fear, cancel self-wrecking resentment, stop secret self-sabotage and stop blaming others for the way you feel.

After reading *Designing Your Own Destiny*, you'll understand why you are perfectly equal to every task you set for yourself, and that you truly can change your life for the better!

1-56718-278-X
mass market, 160 pp., softcover $6.99

Freedom from the Ties that Bind
The Secret of Self Liberation
GUY FINLEY

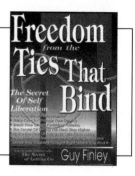

Imagine how your life would flow without the weight of those weary inner voices constantly convincing you that "you can't," or complaining that someone else should be blamed for the way you feel. The weight of the world on your shoulders would be replaced by a bright, new sense of freedom. Fresh, new energies would flow. You could choose to live the way you want. In *Freedom from the Ties that Bind*, Guy Finley reveals hundreds of Celestial, but down-to-earth, secrets of Self-Liberation that show you exactly how to be fully independent, and free of any condition not to your liking. Even the most difficult people won't be able to turn your head or test your temper. Enjoy solid, meaningful relationships founded in conscious choice—not through self-defeating compromise. Learn the secrets of unlocking the door to your own Free Mind. Be empowered to break free of any self-punishing pattern, and make the discovery that who you really are is already everything you've ever wanted to be.

0-87542-217-9
6 x 9, 240 pp., softcover $10.00

To order, call 1-800-THE MOON
Prices subject to change

The Secret of Letting Go
GUY FINLEY

Whether you need to let go of a painful heartache, a destructive habit, a frightening worry or a nagging discontent, *The Secret of Letting Go* shows you how to call upon your own hidden powers and how they can take you through and beyond any challenge or problem. This book reveals the secret source of a brand-new kind of inner strength.

In the light of your new and higher self-understanding, emotional difficulties such as loneliness, fear, anxiety and frustration fade into nothingness as you happily discover they never really existed in the first place.

With a foreword by Desi Arnaz Jr., and introduction by Dr. Jesse Freeland, *The Secret of Letting Go* is a pleasing balance of questions and answers, illustrative examples, truth tales, and stimulating dialogues that allow the reader to share in the exciting discoveries that lead up to lasting self-liberation.

This is a book for the discriminating, intelligent, and sensitive reader who is looking for real answers.

0-87542-223-3
5¼ x 8, 240 pp., softcover   **$9.95**

To order, call 1-800-THE MOON
Prices subject to change

The Secret Way of Wonder
Insights from the Silence
Guy Finley
Introduction by Desi Arnaz, Jr.

Discover an inner world of wisdom and make miracles happen! Here is a simple yet deeply effective system of illuminating and eliminating the problems of inner mental and emotional life.

The Secret Way of Wonder is an interactive spiritual workbook offering guided practice for self-study. It is about Awakening the Power of Wonder in yourself. A series of 60 "Wonders" (meditations on a variety of subjects: "The Wonder of Change," "The Wonder of Attachments," etc.) will stir you in an indescribable manner. This is a bold and bright new kind of book that gently leads us on a journey of Spiritual Alchemy where the journey itself is the destination ... and the destination is our need to be spiritually whole men and women.

Most of all, you will find out through self investigation that we live in a friendly, intelligent, and living universe that we can reach into and that, more importantly, can reach us.

0-87542-221-7
5¼ x 8, 192 pp., softcover
$9.95